A PARENTS' GUIDE TO

UNDERSTANDING

Children's
DREAMS ·AND·
NIGHTMARES

A PARENTS' GUIDE TO

UNDERSTANDING

Children's
DREAMS ·AND· NIGHTMARES

RECIE SAUNDERS

WHITAKER
HOUSE

A Parents' Guide to Understanding Children's Dreams and Nightmares

Recie.com
DreamsChildren.com
Email: DreamsChildren@Recie.com

ISBN: 978-1-62911-950-2
eBook ISBN: 978-1-62911-951-9
Printed in the United States of America
© 2017 by Recie Saunders

Whitaker House
1030 Hunt Valley Circle
New Kensington, PA 15068
www.whitakerhouse.com

Library of Congress Cataloging-in-Publication Data (Pending)

1 2 3 4 5 6 7 8 9 10 11 ᴜ 24 23 22 21 20 19 18 17

Contents

Foreword

Is there a dreamer in your house? Do you draw a blank when your children wake up with a dream and start asking questions? Some might say dreams are simply nighttime fairy tales. But have you ever considered there might be a message to uncover? This book will help you learn how to respond with confidence when the children in your care share dreams or other spiritual experiences with you.

During his years in ministry, my husband, John Paul Jackson, was known for his ability to understand dreams and visions. The foundational courses he authored came from over thirty years of studying the metaphorical language in the Bible, and his expertise in this area made him known as "the dream guy" in some circles.

Throughout this book, Recie, whom I've known for many years, shares his own experience, research, and insight into the meaning of dreams, while incorporating some of John Paul's teachings related to this significant part of the spiritual realm. Recie addresses dreams and other spiritual encounters children have in a thoughtful, age-appropriate way, helping you and the children in your life embrace dreams with more ease. This book presents dreams like pages in a book, full of adventure and waiting to be read, but infinitely more real than fairy tales. Recie reminds us that children, too, receive dreams from God, and are ripe for spiritual encounters through innocent hearts and childlike faith.

As a former teacher, daycare-center owner, and homeschool parent, how I wish a book like this had been available for parents years earlier! For me, early childhood did not include conversations about God, but that didn't stop my sleep time from coming alive. Dreams were a routine occurrence, but without guidance and training, I had no way to understand what I saw. This informative book prepares you to educate your children about dreams and spiritual experiences from a godly perspective.

Children are influenced by countless voices and opinions outside the home—bombarded by a worldview shaped by media and technology. Could some of your children's dreams actually be influenced by God? If so, wouldn't it only make sense to process and discuss these significant encounters with your child in the privacy and safety of your own home? With this book, children, while at the height of curiosity and learning, can discover the purpose of dreams from a Bible-based view that is untouched by mainstream education or church curriculums.

If you've pondered or asked yourself any of these questions, you'll want to read this book:

+ Do the scenes that play out while children sleep really have special meaning?

+ Can children of all ages, cultures, and religions have significant dreams?

+ Should children be encouraged to talk about their dreams and spiritual experiences?

+ How can parents welcome the questions and overcome the fears that children have about dreams?

+ Can children experience God's power in a dream that transforms their life and destiny?

+ Does God give dreams to guide children, and influence parents' decisions concerning the protection of their child?

Children never tire of asking "why?" That question usually triggers an influx of information and endless opinions, but is there a more *natural* way to connect children with their Creator? Instead of endlessly grasping for answers, could we actually cut through some of the sensory and informational overload our children experience during their formative years by just stopping and listening to a dream they had the night before?

This book will help you value dreams—and maybe set the stage for a child's receptivity to God's truths. Find out how to open another window of opportunity for children to understand the ways of God—whose voice and presence is far superior and more valuable than any other they will encounter. And isn't that what we desire for everybody, at every age? A treasured find at any stage of life!

Are you open to sharing in your child's excitement, expecting something powerful to come from a dream? You can't become a child again, but this book gives examples of how to respond to a child about the "dream world" they experience while sleeping.

You'll also learn:

+ How to enhance children's spiritual eyes and ears by walking through and exploring the dream with them.

+ How to understand the meaning behind dreams, and give your children a handy and valuable spiritual tool they can carry with them into adulthood.

+ How to be better prepared to explain spiritual experiences to children in a relevant and positive manner.

- How to introduce them to the symbolic picture language that captures their attention while asleep.

- How to engage your sons and daughters in conversation about spiritual matters, and prepare them to grasp dream interpretation as they mature.

- How to understand dreams that might boost their spiritual confidence, and be used to help others.

Unlike other phases of childhood, dreaming is something you never outgrow. No law or protest can stop anyone from having a dream. Children can continue to grow in the application of dream interpretation, and this book will help make this lifelong spiritual tool a natural part of your children's life—a tool that doesn't require a warranty, doesn't rust, and doesn't become antiquated and useless. Be sure to take advantage of Recie's training and experience with dreams and dreamers as you consider how dreams can be used to reveal the ways of God to you and your family. Who better than a child's Creator to fill their eyes, ears, and senses with the wonder of dreams!

—*Diane Jackson*

Diane Jackson is the lifelong wife of John Paul Jackson, founder of Streams Ministries and creator of the TV program Dreams & Mysteries, which still airs on the Daystar TV Network. Diane, along with her active and vivid dream life, resides in Fort Worth, Texas.

Introduction

In the year 2000, I took John Paul Jackson's Understanding Dreams and Visions class, because the topic fascinated me. At that time, I was not a dreamer and could not interpret dreams at all; in fact, I could only remember three dreams in my lifetime. After taking the class, I felt wounded, and I wondered, *How come the church never taught me that God uses dreams and visions as one way to communicate to mankind?*

After repenting for my heart issue regarding the church, I started reading, listening to, and devouring Bible passages about dreams, visions, and strange events. A few years later, John Paul hired me at Streams Ministries International, which he founded, to lead the Dream Team outreaches. I took teams of interpreters to the streets to evangelize and interpret people's dreams. I was blessed to travel around the world, teaching and speaking on the Spirit realm. You might say I had a dream job.

On the streets, we told people we were practicing our dream interpretation skills and asked them if they had any dreams they needed help understanding. We soon discovered how little people know about the reality of how God talks to us in dreams.

On one outreach event, Scott, a team member, approached a young woman in her early twenties and her friend and asked them if they had any dreams they'd like interpreted. One of the women shared with him this distressing story:

"When I was a little girl my father left me and my mother. I often cried myself to sleep; during these many nights throughout the year, I had the same dream over and over. In the dream I would fly very high into the big, blue sky, and as I was flying, I saw a rainbow, so I would fly over and above the rainbow and land at the door of this castle.

"I would walk inside, onto a beautiful tile floor. As I continued walking, I would see a man sitting in a big chair. So I would climb up onto the chair and into his lap. He would sing to me a song that gave me comfort while wiping away all of my tears. This dream continued for many years, but as I got older it stopped.

"What do you think it means?" she asked Scott.

"What did the man look like?" he replied.

"Oh, I was not allowed to look at his face."

"Did you know his name?" he asked.

"I called him Kingie."

Scott smiled and asked, "Do you know a king that lives above the rainbow in a castle?"

Tears began to fall from her face. "Do you think it was Him?"

"I know it was Him." Scott went on to share with the two ladies about the Lord's fatherly love, the first step in their salvation process.

This dream seems like it would be simple for the woman to interpret on her own, but it wasn't. I've heard hundreds of such stories of people having dreams or visions involving the presence of God, who is wanting them to know Him in a very personal way. Unfortunately, because of our belief system, we often miss or do not believe that God would want to speak to us as His children in any form, let alone in dreams.

Our gifted generation is designed for the supernatural; they are created for kingdom activity and kingdom purposes. So what's stopping them? It might be us. We, meaning the church as a whole, have not sought to understand the very God-encounters that are a part of our heritage. We are often uneducated, unaware, and unprepared to relate to a super-spiritual generation. Regardless of what we think, children *are* dreaming spiritual dreams—they are having visions and supernatural experiences that neither they, their parents, nor their youth ministers understand. I know this is true because I hear the same questions and concerns everywhere I teach:

+ Why does my child have nightmares and how can I help them?

+ What is real and what is just my child's imagination?

+ Are dreams really from God?

+ What is the difference between dreams and visions?

+ Did my child really see Jesus, or was it an angel or maybe a demon?

+ How do I help my child benefit from their dreams and visions?

It is my hope that this book will answer these questions and serve as a guide to understanding dreams and visions so that parents and those who mentor youth can encourage and facilitate these experiences in the children whom God has entrusted to their care.

Moreover, after reading the real-life stories and advice in this dream guide, you will understand dreams and visions from a biblical foundation—not only to help your own spiritual growth but, more importantly, to help your children develop their gifts and understand the goodness of God that is being manifested through their dreams and visions. Without this understanding, you may easily and unintentionally inhibit their relationship with God and prevent their gifts from being recognized, let alone developed and used. I know this because I have been there, as you will see.

1

Who Wants Kids, Anyway?

We're never gonna have kids," couples tell me. When I ask why not, I hear the same response: "This world is so dark and dangerous. It's not like it was when I was growing up. Back then, you could play outside and not worry about someone kidnapping you or killing you." They conclude, "I don't want to bring kids into a world like this."

I understand their concern. Our culturally-hip media blasts children with the message that every destructive behavior imaginable is tolerable: drugs, alcohol, pornography, witchcraft, you name it. Nothing is sacred. No one is spared. Our kids are at risk from the moment they emerge from the womb, and even before. Since America is no longer a Christian nation, we, as Christians, seem to have lost our collective voice. We feel helpless, benched in the game of life, only able to watch as the world spins out of control.

Yet, even in the midst of this spiritual and moral chaos, Christians should not be afraid to have kids! I respond to Christians around the globe by asking this: "What if Moses's mother or Jesus' mother had thought the same thing?" I would argue that at the time they came into this world, the world was a very dark place—in fact, it was probably even worse then than it is now.

THE BLESSING OF CHILDREN

In Moses's day, the hatred that the Egyptians and the king of Egypt had for the Hebrews was barbaric and inhumane. The Hebrews were worked to exhaustion as slaves, and the Egyptians even tried to stop them from multiplying by throwing all newborns into the Nile. The king gave an edict to the midwives to kill all newborn males:

> *Then the king of Egypt said to the Hebrew midwives, one of whom was named Shiphrah and the other Puah, "When you serve as midwife to the Hebrew women and see them on the birthstool, if it is a son, you shall kill him, but if it is a daughter, she shall live."* (Exodus 1:15–16)

This sounds very similar to a story in the New Testament. When Jesus was still a baby, Herod tried to find and kill Him by commanding the murder of every boy two years old and under who lived in Bethlehem and its surrounding hills. (See Matthew 2:16.) It was a slaughter. Having a baby during Jesus' time in Bethlehem would have been far more dangerous than having one today in America!

The reality is that some of the most influential people were born in of the darkest circumstances. On the news, we see women speak before Congress who survived their planned abortion—a terribly traumatic experience to be born out of, yet they are making a difference for future generations. Helen Keller was born deaf, blind, and dumb at a time when people with disabilities were institutionalized. Yet she earned a Bachelor of Arts degree and became an author and political activist, inspiring millions to overcome their darkness—literally and figuratively.

When hearing about babies who defied the odds of an abortion or disability and are growing healthy and strong, I often say to myself, *I want to see where that child is twenty years from now and see the good that person is doing for others.* And quite often, twenty years later, they are doing just that.

So I ask the would-be parents who are turning down a chance to have children, "What if God wants to give you a Moses or someone who would grow up to find a cure for cancer—and you are saying to Him, 'No'?"

The usual response is silence.

Let's not make the same mistake that King Hezekiah did. In God's valuation, Hezekiah was set above all the other kings in the history of Israel. This means his obedience was even more radical and more pleasing to God than David's obedience. (See 2 Kings 18:5–6.) That's an astounding compliment! But one thing he lacked—he had no passion for the generations that would follow him.

When the prophet Isaiah spoke to Hezekiah in Isaiah 38 of the king's impending death, Hezekiah wept and pleaded with God until He reversed His decree and gave Hezekiah fifteen more years of life.

But when Isaiah later brought Hezekiah a message of destruction about many of his offspring, the king couldn't be bothered. Not one single tear, not a whispered prayer, not an iota of effort invested in the securing of the well-being of subsequent generations of his own family line. He had a total disregard for the future generations, so long as he himself died in peace. (See 2 Kings 20:16–19.)

THE JOEL ARMY

Today, the same mind-set is rampant. Instead of treasuring the awesome responsibility to raise up godly citizens in heaven and earth for future generations, couples are postponing childbearing until their careers are well-established. When children *are* conceived, they are shuffled off to childcare because high income in the present is more desirable than developing a spiritual heritage for the next generation. Moms use TV and handheld devices to entertain their children hour after hour, because it is easier than personally nurturing their minds and spirits. Dads accept promotions, knowing that the hours and the travel schedule will be hard on the family. Or, even more frequently, dads come home from work more focused on relaxing for the evening and watching the game on TV than on nurturing the next generation.

As children grow older, parents give in and allow their kids to do unwholesome things that the parents do not approve of, simply because the parents would rather have short-term peace than vigilantly hold the line against the pressures of an evil society. The anger and the persistent whining of their self-absorbed children transcend the parents' commitment to train up the next generation.

As a result, when we turn on the television, walk the streets of our cities, or speak with the young people in our churches, we soon realize that the young generation is in crisis. They are searching for truth, bound by sin, and growing up in troubled homes. Violence, homosexuality, drugs, depression, suicide, and much more plague their hearts and souls with a hopelessness and despair.

Who will speak true life into the next generation—so hungry for true authenticity and for true spirituality?

The church on the corner tries to do so, but they fail miserably. Why? Because they approach the problem legalistically—through a "do" or "don't do" mentality, ignoring the inward transformation that must come before any outward change. The legalistic mentality results in a religious spirit that focuses on correct behavior instead of honest belief. My daughter and sons actually get physically sick when confronted with a religious spirit—it turns their stomach. I believe most youth have similar reactions. They don't have the vocabulary to explain why this is so; they just know they don't like "religion."

And it's not "religion" that they need. This next generation is created to do great things for God, to restore the testimony of His great name back on the earth, and to usher in the end-time harvest. They don't realize it but they are the Joel army:

> And it shall come to pass afterward, that I will pour out my Spirit on all flesh; your sons and your daughters shall prophesy, your old men shall dream dreams, and your young men shall see visions. Even on the male and female servants in those days I will pour out my Spirit.   (Joel 2:28–29)

They are a spiritually-minded generation that believes God lives *outside* the box, but when they go to church all they see is God *inside* a box. They are a generation that wants to see God move in a powerful way and wants to personally encounter Him, but when they go to church all they see instead are programs and half-hearted believers who take no risks.

It is a difficult time to be sure. A pessimist might even say that this is a generation doomed before it begins. And yet, in spite of all of that, I would argue that this is a critical time. I believe we live in a time of incredible opportunity. It is precisely the intense opposition of the enemy against this generation that gives me hope and brings me to the conclusion that the greater the attack, the greater the anointing. Judging by the advancing forces of darkness directed at our young people, the light intended to shine through them must be incredibly brilliant.

NOT THE FIRST TIME

And it won't be the first time that the Lord has used children to accomplish His supernatural agenda. It's helpful to remember that throughout church history, children have had remarkably prophetic experiences—and they were much more common than we think. By "prophetic," I mean the ability to communicate with God through whatever means God chooses to use.

JOAN OF ARC

One of the earliest and most well-known accounts of children functioning prophetically is that of Joan of Arc, the famed teenage liberator of France. At age thirteen she claimed to have angelic visitations from Michael the archangel. In fact, it was in part her steadfast witness about these heavenly encounters that eventually led to her martyrdom at the hands of those who were not open to the power that was manifesting through this incredible young woman.

JOHN WESLEY

John Wesley (1703–1791), the great revivalist, wrote extensively on the need to keep children in order. He also wrote about children experiencing the conviction of the Holy Spirit in his meetings. For instance, he wrote this account about a meeting where he preached on 2 Timothy 3:5, *"Having a form of godliness, but denying the power thereof"* (KJV):

> May 30, 1759: The power of religion began to be spoke of, the presence of God really filled the place. And while poor sinners felt the sentence of death in their souls, what sounds of distress did I hear! The greatest number of them who cried or fell were men; but some women, and several children, felt the power of the same almighty Spirit, and seemed just sinking into hell.[1]

A year before, he wrote again of children encountering the awesome presence of God:

---

1. Daniel Jennings, The Supernatural Occurrences of John Wesley (Sean Multimedia, 2012), 92–93, http://www.danielrjennings.org/tsoojw2.pdf.

July 30, 1758: I began meeting the children in the afternoon.... I had not spoken long on our natural state before many of them were in tears, and five or six so affected that they could not refrain from crying aloud to God. When I began to pray, their cries increased, so that my voice was soon lost.[2]

JONATHAN EDWARDS

Like Wesley, Jonathan Edwards (1703–1758) was one of the great revivalists in America's history—maybe most famous for his impassioned sermon, "Sinners in the Hands of an Angry God." In recording some of the events he witnessed, Edwards wrote,

Very many little children have been remarkably enlightened, and their hearts wonderfully affected and enlarged, and their mouths opened, expressing themselves in a manner far beyond their years, and to the just astonishment of those which have heard them.[3]

HAROLD ARMSTRONG BAKER

Harold Armstrong (H. A.) Baker (1881–1971) wrote of a revival among orphaned beggar boys at the Adullam Rescue Mission that he and his wife started for street children in Yunnan Province, China:

The morning prayer meeting was lasting longer than usual. The older children left the room one by one to begin their studies in the school-room, while a few of the smaller boys remained on their knees, praying earnestly. The Lord was near; we all felt the presence of the Holy Spirit in our midst. Some who had gone out returned to the room.

---

2. (WJW2:11) Supernatural Occurrences, 97.
3. Jonathan Edwards, The Works of Jonathan Edwards, vol. 1 (Grand Rapids: Christian Classics Ethereal Library), 1585, http:// www.ccel.org/ccel/edwards/works1.pdf.

Such a mighty conviction of sin—a thing for which we had prayed so long—came to all, so much so that with tears streaming from their eyes and arms uplifted they cried out to the Lord for the forgiveness of their sins, which now seemed so black. One after another went down under the mighty power of the Holy Spirit until more than twenty were prostrate on the floor....

Eventually an agonized cry went up, beyond anything I had ever heard or imagined, as in visions the children saw the horrors of hell, the anguish of lost souls, and the indescribable evil power of the devil and his angels. Many witnessed themselves bound and dragged to the very brink of hell. Condemnation for sins and the power of the devil over them became a terrorizing reality. But freedom from this evil power through the grace of the Lord Jesus was just as real. When they experienced this liberating power from the clutches of the evil one, salvation was made as real as condemnation had been. Great joy, laughter, and peace resulted from the knowledge of what they had been saved from. This was a realization I am sure they would never be able to forget.[4]

ROBERTS LIARDON

Roberts Liardon wrote a powerful book about his experience with Jesus as an eight-year-old boy titled *I Saw Heaven*. Today, he has a worldwide ministry helping people grow into a deeply spiritual and real relationship with Jesus. In his introduction, Roberts stresses the importance of dreams and visions in our time:

I believe that as time moves toward the return of Jesus, we will see more and more dreams, visions, and other works of the Holy Spirit. It will become even more important

---

4. H. A. Baker, *Visions Beyond the Veil*, 2nd ed. (New Kensington: Whitaker House, 2006), 23–26.

to know God's Word concerning these supernatural manifestations as well as have the discernment by the Holy Spirit as to what is truly of God.[5]

WINGS TO FLY

These are only a handful of publicized accounts of children expressing their prophetic gift over the ages. In this age, we as parents and youth leaders have a choice: we can sit by as a spectators, watching our lives go by, or we can seize the moment and fulfill one of our primary purposes as parents—to become the spiritual beacons God is calling us to be and teach our children to be the same.

We are not helpless. Our Father always has a plan. If we are willing, He will use us to give our children wings to fly, wings that will carry them with the Spirit of God into their appointed destiny as one of the greatest generations ever born.

---

5. Roberts Liardon, *I Saw Heaven* (Ada, MI: Bethany House Publishers, 1987), 4.

2

God Is Speaking to Our Children

Let the children come to me, and do not hinder them, for to such belongs the kingdom of God.
—Luke 18:16

"The First Time" is an exercise I give students while teaching John Paul Jackson's course, "The Art of Hearing God." I ask every student to break up into groups and answer these four questions:

+ When do you believe is the first time you actually heard God speak to you?

+ How old were you?

+ How old were you when you thought you might have a gift or an ability to hear from God?

✦ Does your family know about this gift?

From young to old, less than 10 percent of students believe they heard God as a child. Most say they heard Him after the age of twenty-five. But as I continue through the course to explain the different ways that God speaks, more and more people start to see that God actually had been speaking to them at a very young age. They just didn't realize it. During the class, students would remember a dream or vision that they had as a child and share what they remembered, asking, "What do you think it means?"

From their dreams or visions, I could see that God was definitely speaking to them. So why did they not see it?

I will answer my question with another question: when was the last sermon you heard teaching from the pulpit on how God speaks through dreams and visions?

Because of this absence of teaching, when we do have dreams and don't know what they mean, we don't place much value on them. In my family, growing up, we just forgot them or categorized them as "pizza dreams"—vivid dreams resulting from eating lots of food before bedtime and sleeping restlessly as a result of indigestion.

Likewise, when my wife and I were parents of young children, we didn't have a grid for understanding our children's dreams and nightmares. Our only step in that direction was to pray for them to stop having the nightmares. We didn't value the message in the dreams and nightmares they were having. The same is true for the great majority of Christian parents.

Interestingly, parents will go to great lengths for their children to learn about God and attend church even if they don't have the same commitment in their own lives. I discovered this while helping to establish church plants. The reason people started coming to these new churches was because they had children who were starting to ask questions about God or because they wanted their children to have a foundation of God in their lives. Our church or Sunday school became the expected place where their children could learn about Him.

We told them stories from the Bible. We taught them to pray before they eat and before they go to bed. We taught them about Jesus and how He came to earth as the Son of God to die on the cross for our sins, and that if we believe in Him and confess our sins and are baptized, we will live in heaven with Him forever. We taught them the Ten Commandments, to obey their parents, to not tell lies, and to not do drugs. We taught important values and rules to follow, but it was all one-way communication. We failed to include the vital teaching that *God wants to talk back*. He wants to visit our children at a very young age and communicate with them, much like the Scripture at the beginning of this chapter: *"Let the little children come to me, and do not hinder them."*

Just as the disciples had to be rebuked by Jesus in that verse because they were hindering the children from coming close to Him, so we as parents and teachers may need to reexamine whether we are keeping kids from drawing close to God. We need to reexamine whether we have missed seeing that God is longing for a relationship with our children, and that He is speaking to them in dreams and visions.

The rubber meets the road when the children start having spiritual experiences that they don't know how to interpret, control, or stop—especially terrifying nightmares. When incredible parents come to me at their wit's end over such a situation, I tell them that the first step to helping our children is accepting the reality that God is speaking to all children, whether they are Christians or non-Christians. Acts 2 says that He will pour out His Spirit on *all* flesh. It does not say, "I will pour my spirit only on adults or only on Christians." Children have an important role to play.

GOD SPEAKS TO OUR CHILDREN IN VISIONS

Remember that visions are literal or real encounters, not metaphorical. For those who think that literally encountering God in visions and dreams started with the Azusa Street revival of the early 1900s, take a peek at what the great preacher John Wesley wrote in his journal in 1739:

> What I have to say touching visions or dreams, is this: I know several persons in whom this great change [from fear, horror and despair to love, joy and peace] was wrought in a dream, or during a strong representation to the eye of their mind, of Christ either on the cross or in the glory....
>
> God does now, as aforetime, give remission of sins and the gift of the Holy Ghost even to us and to our children; yea, and that always suddenly as far as I have known, and often in dreams or in the visions of God. If it be not so, I am found a false witness before God. For these things I do, and by His grace, will testify.[6]

Wesley witnessed the fruit of those who had an encounter with the living God in dreams—not just a great story to tell but changed lives—from condemnation to freedom. This has been happening through the centuries!

THE PROPHET SAMUEL

Take a boy named Samuel who encountered God in a vision about three thousand years ago. Samuel had been serving the Lord with his mentor, Eli, in the tabernacle. At that particular time in history, God was not speaking to people much. But one night *"the lamp of God had not yet gone out, and Samuel was lying down in the temple of the LORD, where the ark of God was"* (1 Samuel 3:3). There, in the tabernacle, Samuel didn't yet know how to hear God:

> *The LORD called Samuel, and he said, "Here I am!" and ran to Eli and said, "Here I am, for you called me."*

---

6. John Wesley, *The Journal of John Wesley*, ed. Percy Livingstone Parker (Christian Classics Ethereal Library). PDF-61, http://www.ccel.org/ccel/wesley/journal.html (accessed April 27, 2017).

But he said, "I did not call; lie down again." So he went and lay down.

And the LORD *called again, "Samuel!"*

And Samuel arose and went to Eli and said, "Here I am, for you called me."

But he said, "I did not call, my son; lie down again."

Now Samuel did not yet know the LORD, *and the word of the* LORD *had not yet been revealed to him.*

And the LORD *called Samuel again the third time. And he arose and went to Eli and said, "Here I am, for you called me."*

Then Eli perceived that the LORD *was calling the boy. Therefore Eli said to Samuel, "Go, lie down, and if he calls you, you shall say, 'Speak,* LORD, *for your servant hears.'" So Samuel went and lay down in his place.*

And the LORD *came and stood, calling as at other times, "Samuel! Samuel!" And Samuel said, "Speak, for your servant hears."*   (1 Samuel 3:4–10)

GARRETT'S DAD

Skeptics will say about this account, "Oh well, Samuel's story happened thousands of years ago, and that's the Old Testament. God doesn't speak to us like that anymore." But He does. Some friends of mine in California, Jim and Dawn, shared a story with me that proves this to be true. This is their story:

> Our son was killed in a motorcycle accident. His former wife Olivia and their two children, Priscilla, eleven, and Garrett, six, had still been very close to our son. He had loved his kids. We were all especially concerned for our grandson Garrett. He did not fully understand the concept of death and started showing signs of destructive anger rising up in him—fits of rage.

Some six months before my son's death, our two grand-children were over visiting for the day when the subject came up about angels. My wife, Dawn, would always use these opportunities to share with the grandchildren about God and hearing His voice. Garrett told us that some-times at night he would hear his name called, and it would scare him because he knew it was not his mom or his sister calling him. Dawn comforted him and read the story of Samuel and Eli.

Two weeks ago, we received a text message. It read, "This morning Garrett came to me and said, 'Mom, last night God called my name and I listened like Nana Dawn said. God told me that he chose my Daddy to stay with him in heaven.'"

Olivia continued, "I knew that it was God because Garrett does not use those terms." From that point for-ward, Garrett's personality changed. His young spirit has been healed by God the Father. Dawn and I took them to dinner two days later and little "G" talked the entire eve-ning about his dad—with a smile on his face.

This story brings tears to my eyes. It sounds familiar to the Scripture we just read of the young boy Samuel who also received a visit from God. So let's look at what was going on leading up to Samuel's encounter with the Lord.

YOUR ROLE IN YOUR CHILD'S DREAM LIFE

His mentor, Eli, had sons who were very wicked. They rebelled against the Lord and ignored their father's admonitions. Samuel, on the other hand, ministered to the Lord and obeyed Eli. While Eli's sons defiled the house of the Lord with no fear of God in them, Samuel kept his heart holy and pure with a healthy fear of the Lord.

What if Samuel's story was the story of your son or daugh-ter—or maybe even you? Today, if your children were like Samuel, they would be considered a prude, a virgin, a boring Jesus freak, and so on. Or you may be teased at your job because you hold fast to Christian values when the rest of your coworkers pressure you to go to the bar with them or watch that seedy movie. But we see that young Samuel never gave in to that kind of peer pressure. He stayed faithful to the Lord.

We can help our children not give in to peer pressures but remain holy and pure before the Lord. We can raise up a new generation who will say no to sin and yes to righteousness. To do this, we need to help our children transition from loving, fearing, and obeying us parents to loving, fearing, and obeying God.

God was in the process of accomplishing that transition with Samuel. We read that *"Samuel was ministering to the LORD in the presence of Eli"* (1 Samuel 3:1). The word *"minister"* here means that he was serving the Lord by doing various religious practices and ceremonies with his father. Samuel had daily responsibilities in the temple that his mentor taught him to do. It would be like us teaching our children to go to church on Sunday, read the Bible, pray, and obey.

Most scholars agree that Samuel was about twelve years old at this time. He had grown up in the presence of the Lord and learned to serve in His tabernacle, yet he did not have a personal experience with God. That is a critical point to keep in mind: teaching our children the routine of church life, although important, does not mean they have a personal relationship with Jesus.

This was certainly true in my life. I attended a Catholic school as a child. I memorized the ritual prayers and performed the ritual duties. Then my mother had a personal encounter with Christ. She got saved and gave her life to Him. She led us to the Lord and, after that, instead of calling ourselves Catholic, we called ourselves Christians. I went to church every Sunday morning and Wednesday night and learned a lot about the God of the Bible. It wasn't until I was about twenty-one years old, though, that I personally encountered Him.

At that moment, He became more than the God of my memorized prayers or the God that I sang to on Sunday morning or the God that I read about in the Bible—the God of Abraham, Isaac, and Jacob. He became the God of Recie, which made Him a real person to me. For the first time, I felt that He cared about me, my life, and my decisions. I have always known that and been taught that—my mom told me that and demonstrated it to me—but I didn't understand it or live in that reality until I experienced it for myself.

We need to help our children not only realize that God cares about their lives, but that He also wants them to experience Him and hear Him. That is exactly what this coming generation wants—to experience God. In turn, God wants to move in and through them in a powerful way.

When we read the story of young Samuel, we see that Eli almost missed the opportunity to teach Samuel that God was the one calling his name. When Samuel heard his name called, he came to Eli on three different occasions, thinking it was Eli calling him. Finally, we read that *"Eli perceived that the Lord was calling the boy. Therefore Eli said to Samuel, 'Go, lie down and if he calls you, you shall say, "Speak, Lord, for your servant hears"'"* (1 Samuel 3:9).

God actually *"came and stood"* in Samuel's vision and gave him a very important message about Eli's household: God was going to punish him for not restraining his wicked sons. Naturally, *"Samuel was afraid to tell the vision to Eli"* (verse 15). Similarly, our children will likely be afraid to tell their visions to us, but that is exactly how God decided to speak to young Samuel—in a vision. And that is how God may be speaking to your child. He may be speaking to them about their lives, about their destinies, and about issues going on in their lives.

GOD SPEAKS TO OUR CHILDREN IN DREAMS

God not only speaks to children through visions, but also through dreams. Let's look at a seventeen-year-old boy in the Bible named Joseph whom God also spoke to—this time through metaphoric imagery in a dream.

Now Joseph had a dream, and when he told it to his brothers they hated him even more. He said to them, "Hear this dream that I have dreamed: Behold, we were binding sheaves [bundles of grain] in the field, and behold, my sheaf arose and stood upright. And behold, your sheaves gathered around it and bowed down to my sheaf." His brothers said to him, "Are you indeed to reign over us? Or are you indeed to rule over us?" So they hated him even more for his dreams and for his words.

Then he dreamed another dream and told it to his brothers and said, "Behold, I have dreamed another dream. Behold, the sun, the moon, and eleven stars were bowing down to me." But when he told it to his father and to his brothers, his father rebuked him and said to him, "What is this dream that you have dreamed? Shall I and your mother and your brothers indeed come to bow ourselves to the ground before you?" And his brothers were jealous of him, but his father kept the saying in mind.   (Genesis 37:5–11)

Joseph was the youngest of a large family. Just before this account of the dreams, we read in Genesis 37:3–4 that Joseph was loved by his father more than all the other children because Joseph had been born in Jacob's old age. His father even made him a tunic of many colors that indicated a favored position in his father's eyes. Unfortunately, the tunic caused such strong jealousy and resentment in his brothers that they could not even speak peaceably to him. With all of this going on in Joseph's life, God speaks metaphorically to him in a dream—not once but twice—about his future and his destiny.

If God would speak to a seventeen-year-old boy about his future, don't you think that God wants and is speaking to your children at a young age about *their* future? I know He is because I've heard enough accounts to realize it's true.

Scott, my dream-team member, and I were in Las Vegas interpreting dreams on the street and stopped a young man who was still attending college. The young man shared a recurring childhood dream. In the dream, his friends would come to his home and fall into a black hole at his door on his front porch. Each time in the dream, he would decide to get a crane and lower himself down and rescue his friends.

Scott asked him what he was studying to be in college, and the young man said, "A helicopter rescue pilot." Scott then knew that the crane represented his education. From the young age of twelve and beyond, God had been speaking to this young man about his destiny.

OTHER WAYS GOD SPEAKS

We read how God spoke to young Samuel about the destiny of Eli and his sons in a vision while he was sleeping. We also read how, twice, God spoke metaphorically in dreams to young Joseph as he slept.

What are some of the others ways God can speak to us? Here are a few among many, along with Scriptural support:

AUDIBLE VOICE

"Father, glorify your name." Then a voice came from heaven: "I have glorified it, and I will glorify it again." (John 12:28)

PERSONAL ENCOUNTER

He approached Damascus, and suddenly a light from heaven shone around him. And falling to the ground he heard a voice saying to him, "Saul, Saul, why are you persecuting me?"

And he said, "Who are you, Lord?"

And he said, "I am Jesus, whom you are persecuting. But rise and enter the city, and you will be told what you are to do."

(Acts 9:3–6)

ANGELIC VISITATIONS

Are they not all ministering spirits sent out to serve for the sake of those who are to inherit salvation?   (Hebrews 1:14)

HIS WORD

All Scripture is breathed out by God and profitable for teaching, for reproof, for correction, and for training in righteousness.   (2 Timothy 3:16)

STILL SMALL VOICE

After the earthquake a fire, but the LORD was not in the fire. And after the fire the sound of a low whisper.

(1 Kings 19:12)

God may speak to us in any one or a combination of ways. It's up to us to recognize Him and then hear Him. Let's uncover what those scary night dreams are all about.

3

Overcoming Obstacles to Hearing God

Indeed God speaks once, or twice, yet no one notices it.
In a dream, a vision of the night, when sound sleep falls on
men, while they slumber in their beds,
then He opens the ears of men, and seals their instruction.
—Job 33:14–16 (NASB)

God *does* speak to us, and often not just once or even twice but in many ways, yet we do not perceive Him. Let me give you an example: say that God has been trying to speak to you about a particular issue in your life, such as anger, unforgiveness, resentment, job distress, or relationship conflict. He may be trying to speak to you in a still small voice, yet you do not hear it; through His Word, yet you do not understand it; through a leader's teaching at church, yet you do not perceive it; or through the wise counsel of friends and family, yet you did not realize it.

We have such a hard time hearing God when we are awake, how can anyone expect to hear God when we are asleep? But Job 33 says that when we lay our heads on our pillow at night, He opens our ears and speaks to us in a dream or vision.

So many times in my life, I had an issue with someone that developed into resentment or unforgiveness in my heart. On many of these occasions, God was trying to speak to me through a still small voice, and I ignored it or thought it was not the Lord. Then my wife mentioned something like, "I think you have some unresolved bitterness in your heart toward your friend," but I justified it and told her, "My heart is good toward him."

The next time I went to church, the minister spoke on dealing with resentment and unforgiveness. I said to myself, *Man, I wish my friend could hear this message. He really needs it!* Again, I was not perceiving that God had been trying to speak to me. Then, one night, when I lay my head on the pillow and went to sleep, He opened my ear and spoke to me in a dream. In that dream, I took my car to a mechanic who, after inspecting it, said, "Did you know you were about to have a blowout? If you don't get this fixed you will have one."

I knew instantly in the dream that the Lord was addressing my resentment and unforgiveness and letting me know I was headed for a blowout. So when I woke up, I stopped resisting Him, thanked the Lord for speaking to me, and asked Him to forgive me for my resentment and unforgiveness toward that person.

Looking back at your life, can you identify a time when you know God was speaking to you but you completely missed it?

The reason that sometimes we can't hear Him when we are awake or dreaming is because our souls are resisting Him. Even in our rebellion, though, God is speaking to us in dreams and visions.

In fact, the Scriptures contain over two hundred and twenty-four references to dreams or visions.

The very first recorded dream in Scripture is Genesis 15:12–16:

> As the sun was going down, a deep sleep fell on Abram. And behold, dreadful and great darkness fell upon him. Then the LORD said to Abram, "Know for certain that your offspring will be sojourners in a land that is not theirs and will be servants there, and they will be afflicted for four hundred years. But I will bring judgment on the nation that they serve, and afterward they shall come out with great possessions. As for you, you shall go to your fathers in peace; you shall be buried in a good old age. And they shall come back here in the fourth generation, for the iniquity of the Amorites is not yet complete."

Through a dream, God spoke to Abraham of a future event: his descendants would be held captive for four hundred years. Do you think God could speak to you about a future event for your life or your children's lives? He did so with my six-year-old son, who woke up one morning, saying, "Daddy, I had a dream that we were moving and we got a new house."

So I said, "Ok, let's record the dream in your dream journal and see what happens."

A year later, I got a job at Streams Ministries, and we moved to a new house in New Hampshire. I reminded my son about his dream, and we went to his journal and reread the dream. If nothing else, my son saw that God did, indeed, speak to him in a dream.

After God spoke to Abraham in a dream, He visited many others with important messages:

+ A king encounters God's mercy in Genesis 20:6.

+ In Genesis 31, ten divine instructions are given to Jacob through a dream.

+ In Genesis 37, Joseph has dreams about ruling and reigning over his brothers.

+ In Judges 7:13–14, Gideon gets courage through a dream.

+ The New Testament is full of encounters with God in dreams and visions as well:

+ *And her husband Joseph, being a just man and unwilling to put her to shame, resolved to divorce her quietly. But as he considered these things, behold, an angel of the Lord appeared to him in a dream, saying, "Joseph, son of David, do not fear to take Mary as your wife, for that which is conceived in her is from the Holy Spirit. She will bear a son, and you shall call his name Jesus, for he will save his people from their sins."* (Matthew 1:19–21)

+ The wise men, after visiting baby Jesus, were warned not to return to Herod. (See Matthew 2:12.)

+ Joseph is told to take Jesus to Egypt because Herod is looking to destroy him. (See Matthew 2:13.)

+ The Lord again speaks to Joseph in a dream, telling him that Herod is dead so he can take Jesus back to Israel. (See Matthew 2:19.)

If God gave directions and warnings in dreams and visions to Abraham, Jacob, Gideon, Joseph, and Samuel, do you think it possible that He would give you or your child a direction or perhaps a warning about impending danger?

Absolutely.

This became crystal clear to us after we moved to Fort Worth, Texas, from New Hampshire. We were glad to see the kids making new friends. Michael Ray started hanging out and playing with one particular boy that I had some concerns about. I had to go on a ministry trip, so my wife stayed home with the kids. On my trip I dreamt that I was in a little boy's room that I never saw before. I looked around and saw some very dark things that really concerned me. I wondered, "Whose room is this?"

A voice answered, "In a few days this boy will invite Michael Ray to have a sleepover. Don't let this happen because Michael Ray will lose the innocence in his heart, and you will never get that back."

I woke up shocked and very concerned, so I called my wife and told her the dream and said, "If this boy calls, do not let Michael Ray have a sleepover."

She said, "Okay," and we started to cover this in prayer. Just as the dream said, this boy called and asked if Michael Ray could have a sleepover. My wife didn't give a reason, she just said no. But the little boy was persistent. For weeks he kept calling and asking. My wife felt bad saying no all the time, so we decided to tell him that he could come over and play with Michael Ray anytime at our house but Michal Ray could not go over there.

There is a saying: "The greater the clarity, the greater the cost." God spoke clearly to me because it was going to cost Michael Ray a lot. We had been picking up some clues about this little boy but we brushed them off, saying, "It's nothing." We justified what we were sensing, and thankfully I had the training and experience to perceive God's voice.

Back to Job 33:14–17: *"God speaks once, or twice, yet no one notices it. In a dream, a vision of the night, when sound sleep falls on men, while they slumber in their beds, then He opens the ears of men, and seals their instruction"* (NASB).

Thank you, Lord, for opening my ears and instructing me.

Here again, we see that dreams and visions are God's way of making himself known to us. In Numbers 12:6, the Lord said, *"Hear now My words: If there is a prophet among you, I, the LORD, make myself known to him in a vision. I speak with him in a dream"* (NASB). God is making himself known to us in dreams and visions.

I love this piece in Rick Joyner's book, *The Final Quest*, about God's presence in our dreams:

The Father gave men dreams to help them see the door to his dwelling place. He will only dwell in men's hearts, and dreams can be a door to your heart, which will lead you to him. This is why his angels so often appear to men in their dreams. In dreams they can bypass the fallen mind of man and go straight to his heart.[7]

Dreams bypass man's mind (which is part of the soul) and speak to his heart. But what about nightmares? Do they have a purpose, or are they only distorted dreams? Let's take a look at that next.

---

7. Rick Joyner, *The Final Quest* (Charlotte: Morningstar Publications, 1977), 44.

4

Nightmares and Night Terrors

No matter where I travel in the world or what ethnic group I talk with, I hear a lot of the same comments: "I used to have nightmares when I was a child and was afraid to go to sleep." Or this: "My children are having nightmares, and we don't know what to do."

Different cultures use different methods to help them ward off these nightmares. Native Americans, for instance, hang a dreamcatcher at the end of their beds so that the bad dreams are caught in the web while the good dreams pass through. In Guatemala, worry dolls are small, colorful figures that are thought to keep negative thoughts and nightmares at bay. According to legend, if a child expresses concerns directly to the doll before bedtime, the doll will worry in their place so they can sleep peacefully. Germanic people would plug the keyholes of their bedroom doors to prevent evil spirits from getting through during the night.

But there are more effective, biblical ways to deal with this spiritual threat.

WHAT IS A NIGHTMARE?

Let's look first at what a nightmare or night terror is, what the difference is, and why we are having them. From the secular perspective, the historic use of the term "nightmare" was the original term for the state currently called "sleep paralysis," associated with rapid eye movement (REM) sleep. That definition was codified by Dr. Samuel Johnson in his work, *A Dictionary of the English Language.* Such nightmares were widely considered to be the efforts of demons and more specifically incubi, which were thought to sit on the chests of sleepers.

A nightmare is a dream or even a vision that causes panic, fear, despair, or anxiety due to situations that place them in seeming danger, physical or psychological. These dreams are remembered after waking, and often the person cannot or will not go back to sleep.

The Encyclopedia of Children's Health tells us that nightmares occur during the rapid eye movement (REM) stage of sleep and typically include dreams "of abandonment; of being lost; of falling; or being chased, bitten, or eaten by a monster or hostile animal."[8] Nightmares occur in children as young as eighteen months, but children don't recognize that their encounters in nightmares are not real until the age of three or four years old. A study conducted by Clinical Child Psychology in 2000 found that 95 percent of seven to nine-year-olds have nightmares with less occurring in younger and older ages.[9]

In addition to nightmares, another traumatic phenomenon called night terrors can haunt our sleep. During a night terror, we

---

8. http://www.healthofchildren.com/N-O/Nightmares.html (accessed September 6, 2017).
9. Clare Hanrahan, "Nightmares," *Gale Encyclopedia of Children's Health: Infancy through Adolescence,* 2006, http:// www.encyclopedia.com/doc/1G2-3447200403.html.

are not fully asleep nor fully awake. This is what is called "twilight"—that in-between place. And unlike nightmares, night terrors are not recalled dreams. Children that I have talked with over the years, and even many adults, have recounted the same story to me of times they were sleeping and tried to wake up but could not seem to wake themselves up. They could often feel pressure on their chest or something holding them down and pressing them into their bed, but they could not recall any other details. No matter how much they tried to wake themselves up or even scream for help, they could not come out of this night terror.

WHAT CAUSES NIGHTMARES?

Why would God allow us and even our children to have such nightmares or night terrors?

Quite often, parents tell me, "My child is having nightmares or night terrors and I don't want them to have them anymore."

I respond, "Well, God *wants* your child to have them. Why do you think He is allowing them?" They often look at me like I'm crazy, so I tell them. "He wants them to exercise their authority at a young age."

They are usually shocked to hear something so odd and ask, "What do you mean?"

I conclude, "Scripture is clear that the enemy cannot do anything to us unless he has approval from God."

That still doesn't answer, of course, what would open the door for the enemy to attack you and your children with nightmares and night terrors, even if it's with God's approval. Here are four main causes.

UNREPENTANT SIN

The true meaning of "repent" in the English language is to feel or express sincere regret or remorse. One might also feel sadness, disappointment, and shame at their actions.

However, in the New Testament (such as in Matthew 4:17), "*repent*" means a change of heart or a change of mind. This is the kind of repentance our Lord desires. It will carry us through the rest of our lives while we "*work out our salvation,*" as Paul writes. (See Philippians 2:12.)

So I would say, don't be discouraged. We fall, we get up, we fall again, we get up again. But we are continually taking it to the cross. That is what matters, and that is the whole reason of the cross.

GENERATIONAL SIN

In Numbers 14:18, we see the origin of a generational curse:

The LORD is slow to anger and abounding in steadfast love, forgiving iniquity and transgression, but he will by no means clear the guilty, visiting the iniquity of the fathers on the children, to the third and the fourth generation.

It sounds so unfair for God to punish children for the sins of their fathers! However, there is more to the situation than that. The effects of sin are naturally passed down from one generation to the next. When a father lives a sinful lifestyle, his children are likely to practice the same sinful lifestyle or at least will be tempted to do so. We need not freak out because "*the LORD waits to be gracious to you, and therefore he exalts himself to show mercy to you. For the LORD is a God of justice; blessed are all those who wait for him*" (Isaiah 30:18).

The Lord wants to set us free. He wants to expose the work of the evil one in our lives. I am not immune to generational curses. I was having nightmares and tension in our home for several weeks, which prompted me to ask the Lord, "What's going on? Why is there no peace in my home?" Well, I didn't ask exactly like that. I prayed a simple prayer: "Lord, you are God who knows all and sees all. If there are any generational sins in my family line that are giving the enemy access in my life and my family life, please reveal them to me." Over the next several months I had several dreams speaking about fortunetelling and free masonry in my bloodline. I repented of them and that was the end of it—that easy.

PARENTAL INFLUENCE

Lots of parents don't realize that watching evil things, such as horror movies or pornography, even while their children are sleeping, can give the enemy access to their children through nightmares. Access may also come through personal sins of the parent, occult objects parents bring into the home, or through generational associations, sins, and curses. I am not saying that parents are supposed to be perfect! But neither can we think that we do has no effect upon our children. We need to be watchful and prayerful about the possibility of our own sin causing disruptions for our children.

Moms, who are very fearful by nature, bring their fears into the home. That opens the door to the enemy—who feeds on our fears—to enter her household through nightmares and night terrors in both her and her children.

So, again, don't freak out at scary dreams. Just pray and ask God to show you things in your life that could be a door to them—then shut the door.

One of the things I have discovered in my walk with the Lord is that when you pray and ask God, "What do I need to change?" that prayer is usually answered really quickly. You don't have to fast and pray to get the answer—it usually comes when you least expect it. When the answer comes, resist the temptation to get defensive about it or else you will miss the opportunity to close the door to it.

TEST FOR PROMOTION

God wants us to grow in authority. I have discovered that when we are being spiritually attacked, God's desire is often to have us exercise our spiritual authority over evil so that we grow and get promoted spiritually.

When my sons had a nightmare, they would usually tell me the next morning. One morning Michael Ray told me, "Last night four bears were chasing me and wanted to eat me, so I ran from them. I saw a stick and picked it up and started whacking them on the head and they ran away."

At that moment, Michael Ray grew in his spiritual authority over evil. Whether that evil came to him because of generational sin, an object in the house, unrepentant sin, or testing, I'm not sure. But shortly after that dream he had another one in which he and his older brother Recie got new bikes that were bigger and better, which means that because they exercised their spiritual authority, God promoted them.

Now a sixteen-year-old, Michael Ray had a dream a few nights ago where this dark figure was chasing him and he was afraid. In the dream he stopped and kicked the dark figure and broke its neck. This illustrates my point. I have been training him since he was a little boy to exercise his authority in nightmares and not give any room to fear the evil one. Victory for Michael Ray!

In chapter nine on lucid dreaming, you will learn how your child can gain this authority, too.

5

Discerning Dreams

God does not only speak to Christians in dreams. St Augustine said that God speaks to all of humanity through dreams. Another influential early Church Father, Tertullian of Carthage, said, "Almost the greater part of mankind derives their knowledge of God from dreams."[10] In fact, the internet is full of testimonies from Muslims, Hindus, Buddhists, and many others coming to faith in Jesus due to a dream or vision.

But we must not make the mistake in believing that all dreams and visions are from God. We are called to discern the spirits, even in our dreams. Tertullian put dreams and visions into three categories: those demonically inspired, those that the soul creates, and those that come from God. Understanding these categories will help us to categorize our own dreams as well:

---

10. Tertullian, "A Treatise on the Soul," Chapter XLVII in *Ante-Nicene Fathers*, vol. III, trans. Peter Holmes, https://en.m.wikisource.org/wiki/Ante-Nicene_Fathers/Volume_III/Apologetic/A_Treatise_on_the_Soul/Chapter_XLVII (accessed September 7, 2017).

SOUL-INSPIRED DREAMS

God has given us a clear warning about dreams originating in our own soul:

> *Let not your prophets and your diviners, that be in the midst of you, deceive you, neither harken to your dreams which ye cause to be dreamed. For they prophesy falsely unto you in my name: I have not sent them, said the Lord.*
>
> (Jeremiah 29:8 KJV)

This Scripture is saying that some dreams are brought about by the dreamer, what could be considered the soul—your mind, will and emotions—what you think, what you want, what you feel.

Dreams that you caused to dream or were produced by your soul are usually muted in color. It's sad to say that most people's dream life falls into this category. To the degree that we are ruled and influenced by the soul—mind, will, emotion—we run the risk that our dream, revelation, or interpretation is a creation of the soul.

A gentleman in church was very excited about telling me his dream. "Last night I dreamt that I won the lottery!" he told me enthusiastically.

"Do you play the lottery?" I asked.

"Every week," he said.

"This is not a dream from God," I told him. "It is produced by your own soul—your desires." You should have seen how quickly the joy on his face turned to tragic disappointment.

Our emotions can also rule our dreams. When a mother has her first child, for instance, she sometimes dreams that the child dies by drowning or choking. These dreams are produced by the fearful emotions of her soul. Even so, these dreams should not be ignored. They are a sign that it's time to pray and come out of agreement with fear and into agreement with God's plan for you and your child.

One important truth to realize is that *fear* and *faith* have the same definition: they both believe that something that has not happened is going to happen. What you fear, you empower. When you have fear, you are coming into agreement with Satan's plans. But when you have faith, you are coming into agreement with God's plans.

When your dreams reveal your fears, pray and come out of agreement with that fear and into agreement with faith.

DEMONICALLY-INSPIRED DREAMS

Demonically-inspired dreams are usually black and white or set at night. I will go into more detail in chapter 9 of how to stop these dreams. Here I will simply warn that if there is an area of your life that is not submitted to God and led by the Holy Spirit, then the enemy has a point of access to manipulate your dream life.

GOD-INSPIRED DREAMS

God-inspired dreams, as Tertullian described it, "are honest, holy, prophetic, inspired, instructive, and inviting to virtue."[11] They are usually in full, bright color. They have a spiritual weight to them and often leave you with a feeling that God is speaking to you. Most dreams from God are metaphors and symbolic, so we will need to think symbolically when trying to interpret our dreams.

Proverbs 25:2 says that *"it is the glory of God to conceal a matter. But the glory of kings is to search out a matter"* (NASB). God places great value on us searching for Him. On many occasions, when I had a dream from the Lord, I would spend hours and days seeking Him to understand what that dream meant. Finally, I would get

---

11. Ibid.

some understanding and think, *Wow, for as much time as I put in trying to understand that dream it hasn't actually impacted my life.* Then I would hear the still small voice of the Lord say, "Yeah, but I really enjoyed the time you spent with Me." Sometimes God will give us dreams that perplex us just to spend time with us!

In learning to interpret dreams from God, we have to realize that it's more than just having the necessary tools in our tool-kit. Without God's help, we will not be able to understand our dreams. King Nebuchadnezzar told Daniel that he was able to interpret dreams because the spirit of the holy God was in Daniel. God will not remove our need for the Holy Spirit in this process because dreams from God are infused with his power and his purpose.

God may choose to give us the interpretation of our dreams in several ways. One is by instantaneously revealing the meaning of a dream or vision through an angel, as God did with Daniel. (See Daniel 10:10–15.) Another is by speaking the interpretation to us as we sleep.

We can help our spiritual ears to hear God interpret a dream for us by writing down "all the works," said David.

> *All this he made clear to me in writing from the hand of the LORD, all the work to be done according to the plan.*
> (1 Chronicles 28:19)

On many occasions when I wake up and wonder, *What does that mean?* I write it down, and in the process of writing, thoughts and revelation start to flow. Understanding often comes to me either about the whole dream or about small bits of the dream. When I go back and review my dreams, more understanding comes. Writing down your children's dreams is part of the toolkit for helping your children interpret their dreams as well. See chapter 7 for more tools.

THE PURPOSE OF OUR DREAMS

Once we discern that God is indeed speaking to us, we need to look for *why* He might be doing so. God communicates with us in dreams and visions for several important reasons:

+ He wants to lead us—remember that God led Joseph in a dream to take baby Jesus to Egypt because King Herod was trying to kill him.

+ He wants to show us the error of our ways and warn us—as in the dream that told me not to let my son Michael Ray sleep over with his friend.

+ He wants to reveal areas of our lives that have not taken on Christ-likeness. This happened to me in a dream in which I was shown future things: I was afraid and scared in the dream and didn't know what to do. At the end of the dream, a voice said, "Recie, these things are going to happen in the future. You have fear in your life, and you will sow fear into everyone in that day. Ask Me to heal your fear of the future and I will, because I want you to be a pillar of strength and faith in that time."

I woke up and spent time asking the Lord to heal me, and He did. He loves us so much. He wants to bring healing and strength into our lives, but many of us are missing these encounters of His purpose and plans for us because we either don't believe that God is speaking to us in dreams or we are still ruled by our soul, and our soul is ruling our dream life. Therefore, when God does give us a dream, we don't value it, we don't write it down, or we simply disregard it as a pizza dream. Remember the biblical principal: he who is faithful with little will be given more. This applies to dreams and visions also.

6

Angels Are Visiting Your Children

One way we know that God has great things in store for our children today is that He has been sending His angels to carry out His work in their lives. Who doesn't like angels? Of course we all do! But how do we know whether they really visiting our children—or even us?

The Bible gives us plenty of reasons to believe that they visit us regularly. In Matthew chapter one, Mary, the mother of Jesus, has a visitation from the angel Gabriel who tells her she will bear God's own son. Later in the chapter, Joseph is told by an angel in a dream to take Mary as his wife even though she's pregnant. Seeing angels was a common occurrence two thousand years ago, and it should still be so today.

ENTERTAINING ANGELS UNAWARES

One day my brother called to say that something happened to his teenage son. The night before, his son had left work around midnight. While on his way home, a large man stepped out into the center of the road and waved him down. He stopped. The man came to the passenger side of the car and asked my nephew if he could have a ride. Before my nephew could answer, the guy jumped in the car.

"Could you take me up the street a few miles and drop me off behind an apartment there?" he asked.

My nephew agreed and pulled back onto the road.

"Can I tell you something?" the guy continued.

"Yeah," my nephew replied.

The guy told my nephew that he needed to get his life right with the Lord. He knew that my nephew had just moved out of his parents' house and was living with a girl and doing drugs. My nephew was shocked and visibly shaken by the conversation. The guy continued, "I know that the Lord loves you and has a plan for your life, so you need to get back on the straight and narrow."

When they arrived at the apartment, the guy asked, "Do you need any gas money?"

"No," my nephew answered.

"You don't understand. I have no use for it." The man got out of the car and disappeared.

My brother asked me what I thought about this event. I said, "Who do you know that uses that terminology with money? 'You don't understand. I have no use for it.' Even people who had loads of money would say, 'No—don't worry about it. I have plenty.'"

After a pause, I told my nephew, "The guy was an angel."

Hebrews 13:2 says that we can entertain angels without being aware of it.

PETER AND THE ANGELS

It's clear that God is coming after this generation in a strong and loving way, and He will do whatever it takes to show people His love for them and rescue them from the clutches of darkness.

Take, for example, Peter's incredible rescue by angels in Acts 12:5–9:

> Peter was kept in prison, but earnest prayer for him was made to God by the church. Now when Herod was about to bring him out, on that very night, Peter was sleeping between two soldiers, bound with two chains, and sentries before the door were guarding the prison. And behold, an angel of the Lord stood next to him, and a light shone in the cell. He struck Peter on the side and woke him, saying, "Get up quickly." And the chains fell off his hands. And the angel said to him, "Dress yourself and put on your sandals." And he did so. And he said to him, "Wrap your cloak around you and follow me." And he went out and followed him. He did not know that what was being done by the angel was real, but thought he was seeing a vision.

Incredibly, Peter could not discern whether or not the angelic encounter was real. He thought he was still dreaming or seeing imaginary visions while awake. How can we discern the difference between a dream, a vision, and reality?

Dreams are metaphoric and very symbolic in imagery. As you sleep, God uses His picture language to communicate a very important message. These images are not meant to be taken literally. We see this in Pharaoh's dream of seeing seven fat cows coming out of the Nile in Genesis 34. There were not literally seven fat cows coming out of the Nile River. They were a metaphor from God about seven years of plenty.

Visions, on the other hand, are real encounters. You can have them when you are awake or when you are asleep. Peter was sleeping when an angel hit him on his side to wake him up; yet, he couldn't discern if this encounter were real or symbolic until verse 10 when he and the angel *"came to the iron gate leading into the city. It opened for them of its own accord."*

Peter finally realized what was happening and said, *"Now I know for sure that the Lord has sent forth His angel and rescued me from the hand of Herod and from all that the Jewish people were expecting"* (Acts 12:11).

With the angel's help, Peter walks out of the jail to the house of fellow believers who were praying. And listen to what happened there:

> *When he realized this* [that his angelic encounter was real], *he went to the house of Mary, the mother of John whose other name was Mark, where many were gathered together and were praying. And when he knocked at the door of the gateway, a servant girl named Rhoda came to answer. When she recognized Peter's voice, in her joy she did not open the gate, but ran in and reported that Peter was standing at the gate. They said to her, "You are out of your mind." But she kept insisting that it was so, and they kept saying, "It is his angel!"*
>
> (verses 12–15)

When the girl named Rhoda looked out the door and saw Peter, she probably screamed and ran upstairs where the disciples were gathered in prayer and said, "Peter is at the gate!" Their response—*"It is his angel!"*—says two things to us today: first, it implies that angels can take on our likeness or that our guardian angels look like us; second, it indicates that angels were so frequent and common, the disciples didn't even feel the need to leave what they were doing to go and see the angel. Consider that for a moment. If you were in a meeting and someone came in and said, "There's an angel in the parking lot," wouldn't most of the people run out of the meeting to see the angel? I would be the first one. I hope the time comes again when angelic sightings are so common they are unremarkable!

CHILDREN SEE ANGELS TOO

I recall a little boy who often saw angels in church services, but when he told his parents, they only commented to each other, saying things like, "Our son sure has a great imagination!" After a while, the child stopped seeing angels.

As parents, we often forget the strength of our words; when we label a child's dream as "imagination," the child believes us and consequently will stop having the very encounters God wants for them. We may not be able to see what our children see, but that doesn't mean it was pure imagination and not "real." Children are innocent and trusting; their young eyes have not grown callused as ours have. They are full of faith because they haven't been taught otherwise.

Sadly, it doesn't take long for this faith to fade. In our science-based, seeing-is-believing society, we often take what comes so naturally to our children and squash it without even realizing what we're doing.

Among those who do understand the spirit realm and welcome the Lord to work through it, angelic visitations are more common than we realize. I have many friends who don't publicly share their angelic visitations; they share them privately. Most of them carry these encounters in their hearts with fear and trembling and would not dare to puff themselves up about it. Likewise, I have had numerous angelic encounters, and my children and wife have had them also.

In 2000, when I first met John Paul Jackson and took his course on dreams and visions and the mystical realm, he told us about a pastor who shared this story about his son: "On many occasions, I have gone into his room and caught him talking to his imaginary friend. I'm not sure how to handle this. Do I tell him to stop? Do I pray against it? Do I cast it out? What should I do?"

John Paul replied, "Did you ask him who he is talking to?"

He said, "No, can I do that?"

John Paul said, "Sure."

The next time the pastor saw his son talking with his imaginary friend, he asked, "Son, who are you talking to?"

The son said, "An angel, Daddy."

The pastor told John Paul, "I did what you said and my son said he is talking with an angel."

John Paul said, "Great! Did you ask him what the angel wanted?"

Again, he replied, "Can I do that?"

John Paul said, "Sure."

So the next time he encountered his son talking with his angel, the pastor said, "Son, ask the angel why I can't see him but you can." The six-year-old boy—that's right, only six years old!—asked the angel. The son then turned to his father and replied, "The angel said it's because your eyes have seen too much evil."

Ugh! Let that sink in for a moment. In fact, just stop and allow the Lord to touch you right now: *Lord, I pray that you would heal our eyes from all the evil that we allowed to come through our eye gates. Cleanse us and help us get to a pure place in you so that we can see holy and pure things again. Amen.*

After getting up off the floor in tears, the pastor said, "Son, ask the angel if I will ever see."

The boy turned to the angel, asked, and said to his father, "He said yes, but it will take time because your callus runs deep."

No wonder the church no longer sees! We have allowed too much filth and evil to go through our eye gates. Jesus said we must become like little children again.

And you have a role now as an adult. When your child has an imaginary friend, don't be afraid to ask: Who are you talking to? What is this imaginary friend telling you? What does he want? It could very well be their imagination, and there is nothing wrong with that. And it could be a not-so-friendly spirit. As their parent, it is your responsibility to accurately discern and identify which realm their friend is in.

John Paul shared privately with me that the first demon he ever saw with his natural eye looked like the character from the movie *ET*. A few years later the movie came out. I wonder why the enemy used Hollywood to make a character that is actually a form of a demon that children would be persuaded to love. Maybe because he wants children to not be afraid of his spirit when it actually visits them in a dream or vision. Just a thought. Remember that Scripture says the enemy is crafty and deceptive: *"Be sober-minded; be watchful. Your adversary the devil prowls around like a roaring lion, seeking someone to devour"* (1 Peter 5:8).

Discerning the origin of spirits is beyond the scope of this book. Yet, it is imperative to study it because my experience tells me that visitations are increasing as we move further into the last days, especially from angels. And we do not want to be like Peter, who didn't even realize *"that what was being done by the angel was real, but thought he was seeing a vision"* (Acts 12:9).

When I started on staff with John Paul in 2000, I would ask a conference crowd how many people have dreams of seeing angels or going to heaven or flying. Only a few hands raised. Over the last fifteen years when I have asked the same question, a lot more hands go up and a lot more questions are asked. Times are changing.

7

If You Don't, the World Will

God is Spirit and, therefore, he communicates to our spirits. It is the ability to hear and understand the language of the Spirit that the church has lost, needs to rediscover, and needs to help our children to discover.

The Hebrews wrote much about how God speaks to us in dreams. Take the example of Joseph in Genesis 37. When sharing his dream with his brothers, he didn't tell them what the interpretation was. They knew what it meant. They understood dreams.

I believe that is what God truly desires for us today, as was clearly seen when a close friend of mine shared a dream that really put into perspective what is going on with the fight for our children and their gift to hear God.

Here is her dream, as I recall her words:

> I was sleeping in my bed and felt a powerful presence enter into my room. I looked up and saw a towering figure

and instinctively knew that this spiritual being was prominent and very important. This being was just standing there staring at me, so I decided to ask him a question:

"Where are we currently in the book of Revelation?"

He said, "I am not at liberty to discuss that," but I continued asking him questions about the end times. To each one, he said "I am not at liberty to discuss that."

So I asked him, "Why are you here?" [which was the right question]

He said, "Are you training your children in the gifts that they have? Because if you don't, the world will."

This dream occurred right after Harry Potter saturated the market with books and then movies, trying to capture our children's spiritual gifts for use on the dark side. It's our responsibility to train our children—not the world's responsibility, and not even the church's. At least that is the way God sees it.

THE IMPORTANCE OF SPIRITUAL EDUCATION

A basic law of the Hebrews found in Deuteronomy 6:7 says, "*You shall teach them* [the words of God] *diligently to your sons and shall talk of them when you sit in your house and when you walk by the way and when you lie down and when you rise up.*" God wants us and our children to understand all of the Bible: we can't just pick and choose what we like and what we don't like.

The Hebrew culture was extremely successful at making God and His Word an important part of life because religious education was life-oriented, not information-oriented. The key to teaching your children to love God is stated clearly in that verse in Deuteronomy. If you want your children to follow God, make God a part of your everyday experiences. Diligently teach your children to see God in all aspects of life—at home, on the road, at bedtime and breakfast time—not just at church.

Psalm 78:5 is also clear that God *"established a testimony in Jacob and appointed a law in Israel, which he commanded our fathers to teach to their children."* God commanded that the stories of his mighty acts in Israel's history be passed on from parents to children. This shows the purpose and importance of spiritual education to help each generation obey God and set their hope on him. It also helps our children keep from repeating the same mistakes as us. What are you doing to pass on the history of God's work to the next generation?

In my many travels of doing hundreds of street festivals over the years, I heard heart-breaking stories from parents in the body of Christ who do not understand their children's gift to hear God in dreams and, therefore, cannot teach them the way they should go. Whenever there is a non-belief theology in the church about a spiritual truth, children and adults find places where they can operate in that truth. That's why Wiccan, New Age, and others spiritual organization are filling up with many of God's children.

On one occasion, my dream team and I were in Nevada's Black Rock Desert for the largest pagan festival in the US—Burning Man. A women in her mid-twenties came to our tent. She wanted to tell us about a recurring dream she had for the last few weeks. She dreamt that she was flying in the air toward the clouds with her index finger pointing up toward the sky, and as she was flying she could see off in the distance an angel flying toward her with its index finger pointing at her. They were about to meet and touch pointing fingers but she woke up. We interpreted that she has a prophetic gift/calling on her life, and it's about to receive a touch from heaven to activate it.

We asked her, "How do you practice your spirituality?"

She said, "I'm into Wiccan." She explained further, "I have always known I had some kind of prophetic gift since I was a little girl. One day I asked my mom, 'When are we moving to Florida?'

"My mom said, 'Honey we are not moving to Florida.'

"A week later I asked my mom again, 'When are we moving to Florida?'

"My mom again said, 'Honey, we are not moving to Florida.'

"A week later I asked my mom again when we were going to move to Florida. This time she was frustrated with me and a little angry and said, 'Honey, this needs to stop! We are not moving to Florida.' Just then my father came home from work, walked in the door and said, 'Honey, I got a promotion at work, and we are moving to Florida.'"

As you can imagine, her mom was a little shaken up and took her to their church pastor. After recounting the whole story to him, he shook his finger at the little girl and said, "This is not of the Lord—it's of the devil, and you need to stop doing this right now." With tears in her eyes, reliving the story, she said, "That's when I turned away from the church, and as I got older went into Wiccan to practice my gift."

This is a sad but true story of many young children being shut down in their spiritual gifts. This is the very reason that I have been wanting to write this book, so that I can help parents understand how to help their children cultivate their gifts and not unintentionally hinder them, even though they may not understand it all right now.

PROTECTING OUR CHILDREN

Some nightmares are spiritual warfare dreams that warn us of a plan of the enemy so that we can intercede against it. Children more typically, however, have nightmares sent by the enemy to frighten them away from spiritual experiences.

Because nightmares and night terrors begin at such an early age, children intentionally shut themselves down and no longer remember their dreams, nor are they open to any kind of supernatural experience, and the enemy wins a small victory.

I hear many testimonies from people who have come to realize that they stopped dreaming as children because of nightmares. It is our job as parents to ensure that the enemy does not win this battle over our children's spiritual lives!

How then can we help protect our kids from the harassment of the enemy during the night season?

CLOSE OFF ACCESS

First, we need to ask ourselves how the enemy gains access to them. What video games do your children play? For instance, I do allow my children to play PlayStation, but I monitor which games they can play.

What movies and TV programs do your children watch and what books do they read? Some are blatantly occult, such as the Harry Potter series. Some are much more subtle. Pocahontas, for instance, introduces children to the idea of many gods when the magical tree advises the free-spirited young lady, "All around you are spirits, child. They live in the earth, the water, the sky. If you listen, they will guide you."

If you watch and listen closely, you will find not only occult themes but intolerance of Christian worldviews in many children's movies that, on the surface, seem so innocent and sweet. The answer to this problem is not to lock your kids in a closet and banish all games and entertainment from the house; I love playing video games and watching movies with my kids! What I am saying is that we need to pay attention to those things that can open doors of access into our children's lives.

So, play, watch, or read with them. When occult themes present themselves, it is a perfect teaching opportunity to stop and discuss what these themes are really trying to teach them and why following that teaching leads to death and destruction. It's also the perfect time to teach what God's way is and why following his path leads to life and blessing. If you aren't sure if something is occult or not, it is a good time to seek the Father for wisdom and discernment. When speaking at a church in Texas, a mom came to me with her thirteen-year-old daughter and said the girl was having bad nightmares and was afraid to go to sleep. So we talked about what was going on in her life, about the games she played, what movies she was watching, and what items mom and dad had in the house. She had no idea what could be opening the door to these nightmares. I looked at the young girl who appeared quite lethargic, even sickly. Her mom asked if I would pray for her to get better because she had not been feeling well, so I did. No response came, and I did not have any revelation about what was happening to her.

Break time came upon us, and I walked with the pastor to his car for our lunch appointment. Before opening the car door, I glanced into the car next to me and saw the mother that I had just talked with. In between her seat I noticed a Harry Potter book. I told the pastor that if he and his wife would sit down with the family, pray for them, and ask them to throw away the book, the child would get better and stop having nightmares. I received an email about two weeks later saying they did what I recommended; the girl's sickness went away and the nightmares stopped.

It's time to clean house. If you don't find anything that evil spirits can gain access through, then you have to ask yourself, "What is being allowed into the house another way, even through me?" Leave no stone unturned in your search for the source of access.

PRAY OVER YOUR CHILDREN

In addition to closing off access, you need to pray over your children every night. I would pray each night with my kids when they were young that God would open their eyes and give them dreams from him that would comfort them. I helped my children access God's comfort through lucid dreaming.

In this next chapter I will be dealing with how I taught my children to exercise their authority in a nightmare or night terror even at the young ages of five and six. If our children are learning to exercise their spiritual authority over evil in a nightmare or night terror at such an early age, they will be prepared to exercise their authority at critical times throughout their lives. When they enter their teenage years, for instance, they will be better equipped to say no to sin and yes to righteousness. Moreover, ever since I taught them this, the frequency of their nightmares and night terrors reduced greatly.

A CAVEAT

One caveat before closing: please don't get religious about the advice in these chapters. What I mean is that I don't believe that you must do exactly the same thing with your children that God is telling me to do about mine. I have had many parents tell me, "I don't let my kids play PlayStation and you shouldn't either." I would simply respond that every child is different, so we need to ask the Lord what He wants and what He will allow for the children that He put in our care. If God is speaking to you to not let your kids play PlayStation or watch certain movies with you, then amen! I am with you. But please don't put that on other parents or children. I just needed to say that!

8

Teaching the Gift

As we saw in the last chapter, we as parents have to be so careful to not shut down our children as they learn to exercise their gifts, lest they turn from God toward other means of spirituality that are very willing to guide them into all forms of occult practices.

When I first learned about the reality of communicating with God through dreams, I realized the mainstream church was not going to teach my children how important dreams are for today as they were in biblical days. So I asked the Lord to show me my children's gifts, especially their ability to communicate with Him. I also knew I had to start encouraging them in developing their gifts.

We can encourage our children by speaking positive statements about their gifts and not giving up on them, even when they frustrate us. This is equally true in their everyday life as it is in their dream life. To show how this is true, I'm going to share a story about the power of words over a situation in my son's life.

When I first moved to New Hampshire, I was backing our jeep out of the driveway and did not see Li'l Recie's bicycle. I ran over it, breaking his training wheels off the bike. I said to him, "Well, today is your lucky day—you're going to learn how to ride without training wheels."

He said, "Okay!" Very excited, he started riding as I held the back of his seat, guiding him down the driveway while also helping him keep his balance. He wobbled all over the place. I did this several times and said, "Keep practicing and you'll get better." Later that day he came in crying, telling us he couldn't do it. He wanted his training wheels back on. I said, "Recie, your training wheels are broken, and I can't fix them. You're going to have to learn how to ride without training wheels."

After several attempts throughout the day, he said, "I'll try again tomorrow." Well, tomorrow came and he fell really hard, scraping up his knee and hands. He came in crying and said, "Dad, I don't want to learn. It's too hard."

I said, "Son, you can do it and I believe in you." So he kept trying and fell again. This time we thought he broke his color bone. We took him to the doctor who, fortunately, told us all he did was bruise it. The discouragement caught on. Michael Ray, his brother, came up to me and said, "I don't want my training wheels off because I don't want to hurt my shoulder like Recie."

This is the critical moment in the story where Recie and his brother could have adopted a spirit of fear and hopelessness or courage and perseverance. After a couple of days, Li'l Recie got back on his bike and tried again—only to come in crying that he couldn't do it. I said to him, "Recie, I believe that you can do it, and if you won't quit and keep trying by the end of the week, you will not fall again—you'll be riding all by yourself."

As I watched him, he seemed determined to learn. A couple of days later, I came home to see him riding his bike with a big smile and attitude of accomplishment. I got out of the car and said,

"Recie, you did it! You're riding your bike." He looked up at me and said, "Dad, you said that if I kept practicing and didn't quit, by the end of the week I would be riding without falling." Wow! A few minutes later I looked out the window and saw Li'l Recie trying to teach his little brother how to ride his bike. He did exactly what I did—he walked beside Michael Ray, holding on to the back of the seat. What an endearing and proud picture for a father to see.

On the other hand, what if I would have said, "Son, your problem is your attitude. When I was your age I learned to ride my bike in a week." Or "When your sister was your age, she learned in two days and she's a girl." Or what if I would have said, "Son, maybe you're still mad at me and have some unforgiveness in your heart toward me because I ran over your bike."

If I had chosen any one of those responses, it would have completely shut him down. Yet, this is how we've responded in the church with people who have moved and operated in spiritual encounters or dreams and visions. We have shut them down instead of helping them learn how to ride that bike and work with them through the process.

Li'l Recie struggled with the same issues we struggle with today: "Maybe I'm not good enough or maybe I'm not called to ride a bike." The enemy was feeding him lies, telling him he's a failure and that he'll never accomplish riding a bike.

He expressed these lies by saying, "It hurts so bad. I can't do it anymore." Recie even got that idea deep into his soul, telling himself, "I don't want to hurt anymore. I can't do it." But the words that overcame all these words of death were the words of his very own dad: "If you don't quit but keep trying, you will be riding your bike in a few days."

If we don't allow our children to quit but keep trying, they will be operating in their talents, skills and spiritual gifts, including hearing God, much sooner than later. Let us not shut something spiritual down because we don't understand it. Study, listen to tapes, read biblically-based books that effectively deal with and encourage you to overcome the frustrating situation you are facing.

TEACHING YOUR CHILDREN TO HEAR THAT STILL SMALL VOICE

Once we have encouraged our children to hear God and not dismiss Him, how do we help our children actually hear His still small voice? This is probably the most difficult and frustrating thing for children to discern because they don't know if what they are hearing is their own thoughts or the Holy Spirit speaking to them.

In teaching that discernment to my children, I played games with them. These games were to teach our children to learn to listen to the Holy Spirit, not to see who had the better gift to hear. They also weren't guessing games. We prayed and asked the Lord to teach us. Before playing, I would say, "Let's play a game and ask God to speak to us so we can learn how to hear His still small voice."

One of the games we would play is "Pick a number between 1 and 10." One person would pick a number and write it down and the others would ask God to show them what number it was. They had to learn to discern which voice is God's and which voice origi-nates in their own thoughts.

We would also play games like "What room am I thinking about in our house?" We would sometimes play these games on our bed before bedtime for hours. As the children grew older, I changed up the games. We would watch TV game shows, ask the Holy Spirit to show us who is going to win, and then we'd each pick who we thought was going to win.

As they grew older, we increased the difficulty, such as asking God to show us what would be the next song to play on the radio or what the final score of a football game would be. You may think these are carnal requests, but God wants us to learn to hear Him, and games are a great way to help our children begin to learn to hear the Holy Spirit.

If they had dreamed of winning one of these games and gaining truckloads of fame and fortune, that would likely be a result of their own soulish desires. But earnestly seeking the Lord's voice while awake is a godly pursuit. It also make for good family time.

While teaching my kids how to hear God, we were living in New Hampshire and I was still teaching the dreams course. One particular morning, my wife drove me to work before taking the kids to school. While on the way to work, my son, Li'l Recie, who was six years old, blurted out, "Mommy, you're going to get into a car accident today."

Instead of stopping and praying, I did the opposite. I said, "Recie, don't put that into the air. Mommy is not going to have an accident today." Sure enough, not five minutes after she dropped me off at Streams Ministry, she slid on the ice and hit a tree. Fortunately, she hit it at the only place on the car where no one was sitting, so no one was injured.

Little Recie heard that still small voice that comes like a butterfly and lands on your shoulder—if you don't immediately recognize it, it soon flies away. I apologized to him for not valuing his gift in hearing the Lord. For certain, he will never forget that he heard him at such a young age. Li'l Recie even tried to explain to us why God let the accident happen: "God doesn't slip, Mom. God must have turned to say something to an angel, and when he looked back at you driving, he saw you sliding on the ice. So he turned the car to hit the tree where no one was sitting."

In another example, I received an email in April 2012 from a parent whose child seems to be clearly hearing that voice, and the parents don't know what to do:

> I am writing this email seeking help for my six-year-old son. Recently he has begun to experience things that I do

not have the knowledge and assistance to help him with. He is afraid to go outside because he hears the sound of bombs dropping. He is terrified of President Obama, saying, "He is going to hurt us." Understand, we are not overtly political people, and there is no frame of reference for him to think this. He is also praying for God to take him to heaven. He is afraid of what is going to happen here and wants to be in heaven.

Every day he prays for God to take him NOW, knowing that he will not see his family any longer. He also talks about a war going on; he looks off in the distance and says there is a war going on over there. I do not know where this is coming from, what is happening to him and how to help him.

A pastor friend recommended that I visit your website. I am not sure who responds to this email, but we are desperate for someone to guide and direct us. Someone referred us to a website about Crystal Children, but it was extremely new age and did not line up with our theology. Please if you can offer us any advice, please contact us.

Here is my response:

This is difficult. The child is gifted, but how to handle the gift and the child involves the personality God has given the Child. The parents must become confident that they have been chosen by God to parent this child. They are not lacking in ability—they may be lacking in understanding, but aren't we all?

God felt they could, with the help of those He has put around them, lead this child to the greatest purpose for which God created this child. If the parents fear failure, that fear will translate to the child as "fear of tomorrow" and the child's fear will become worse. Overall, the parents must convince the child that

+ God really loves them
+ The family needs him (the child)
+ God will use the child to help the family and others
+ What they see is not here yet
+ God will protect them
+ God will prepare them
+ God will lead them to safety
+ This gift will help many others

This advice can be applied to our lives as well. God really loves us, our families need us, God will use us to help our family and others, what we see is not here yet, God will protect us, God will prepare us, God will lead us to safety, and our gift will help many others.

Again, we serve a God who longs to have a relationship with us, and He will come to us in many different ways to communicate to us while awake and asleep, in young and in old.

ENCOURAGEMENT TOOLKIT

To encourage your child to welcome encounters with God in a spiritually discerning way, an encouragement toolkit is a must.

BIBLICAL STORIES

One helpful tool is to become familiar with examples in Scripture that match the child's experience and then discuss it with them. For instance, if your child is having dreams or visions of our Lord reaching out to him or her in some way, the experience of the little Samuel will greatly encourage your child to accept his call.

Recall in chapter 3, I told of a boy named Garrett who lost his father in a motorcycle accident, and of his grandmother, who read Scripture to Garrett about how Samuel heard someone calling his name three times. His father, Eli, told Samuel if he hears his name called again, to say, "Here I am Lord."

Samuel did that and had a wonderful personal experience with the Lord.

JOURNALING AND PRAYER

Journaling is another great way to talk about dreams and spiritual experiences and demonstrate that we value them. When my sons wake up after having a dream, my wife or I record it for them in their dream journal. Even though I have interpreted thousands of dreams, I sometimes have no clue what theirs mean. Still, we write the dream down and continue to ask God for the interpretation. As is recorded in Genesis 41, where Joseph says to Pharaoh about his dream, in effect, "The interpretation belongs to God."

In a nutshell, here are some of the ways parents can help their children remember dreams and glean some meaning from them:

+ Pray to God and the Holy Spirit for guidance and truth.

+ Tell related Bible stories.

+ Write down their dreams in a dedicated dream journal (such as the one included at the end of this book!).

+ Have your children draw pictures of their dreams.

+ Have them act out their dreams (this can be really hilarious for the whole family).

+ Try to interpret their dreams; keep it simple, and if desired, use the dream dictionary included at the end of this book for reference.

+ Review their dreams every six months.

As you and your child pray, write, draw, act, interpret and review, connections will be made that may otherwise be missed. Write down these connections or related thoughts in the journal. Pray about the interpretation some more and review the dream and those connections again in six months. Sometimes life events will make the interpretation tangibly clear and call you back to the journal to see how the dream revealed itself in your child's life. Write that down as well. This process will sharpen your interpretation skills and both you and child will grow in discernment and spiritual strength.

Of course, this might be easy to do with dreams about Sponge Bob or Superman but not so easy when it comes to nightmares. Yet these dreams can be the most spiritually powerful training sessions your child will ever have asleep or awake. So, don't fear.

9

Controlling the Game with Lucid Dreaming

Nightmares don't have to terrorize your children; in fact, they can actually help your children gain victory over evil through a form of dreaming called lucid dreams. In the simplest terms, a lucid dream is one in which you are aware that you are dreaming. Most commonly, it's when you have a dream, wake up, think about the dream, and go back to sleep, and right back into the dream. The term itself was coined by the Dutch psychiatrist and writer Frederik Van Eeden in 1913.

Even though lucid dreaming has only come to the attention of the general public in the last century, it is not a modern discovery. We can see an early example of a lucid dream through a letter written by St. Augustine to a priest by the name of Evodius in AD 415. In the letter, Augustine describes the lucid dream experiences of

Gennadius, a physician from Carthage. Gennadius, plagued with doubts as to whether life existed after death, sought God on the matter, and God answered his sincere inquiry in a lucid dream:

> There appeared to him in sleep a youth of remarkable appearance and commanding presence, who said to him: "Follow me." Following him, he came to a city where he began to hear on the right hand sounds of a melody so exquisitely sweet so as to surpass anything he had ever heard. When he inquired what it was, his guide said: "It is the hymn of the blessed and the holy."[12]

At this point Gennadius woke up and thought nothing more of it than a dream. In today's language we would call that a pizza dream. Or we'd say, "I should not have watched that movie last night," or "That was just my imaginations." But God persisted and appeared to him again the next night.

> The same youth appeared to Gennadius and asked whether he recognized him, to which he replied that he knew him well, without the slightest uncertainty.... On this the youth inquired whether it was in sleep or when awake that he had seen [the vision of heaven].
>
> Gennadius answered: "In sleep."
>
> The youth then said: "You remember it well; it is true that you saw these things in sleep, but I would have you know that even now you are seeing in sleep."...
>
> The teacher went on to say: "Where is your body now?"
>
> He answered, "In my bed."
>
> "Do you know that the eyes in this body of yours are now bound and closed, and that with these eyes you are seeing nothing?"

---

12. William John Sparrow-Simpson, "Letter 159 (AD 415)" in The Letters of St. Augustine, 1026, https://books.google.com.

"I know it." [With this awareness, we see that he was lucid dreaming]

"What then are the eyes with which you see me?"

At this point, Gennadius stayed silent. The youth then told him the answer he was seeking:

> "As while you are asleep and lying on your bed, these eyes of your body are now unemployed and doing nothing and yet you have eyes with which you behold me and enjoy this vision. So after your death, while your bodily eyes shall be wholly inactive, there shall be in you a life by which you shall live, and a faculty of perception by which you shall still perceive. Beware, therefore, after this of harboring doubts as to whether the life of man shall continue after death."

This believer says that by this means, all doubts as to the matter were removed from him. By whom was he taught this but by the merciful providential care of God.[13]

Lucid dreaming—consciously interacting with the people and events in a dream—is very powerful. That is one of the reasons why dark forces don't want us to believe or value it, and why it has not been taught in seminaries or the church. For example, *The International Standard Bible Encyclopedia*, which is used in Bible schools and seminaries gives us a big clue as to why dreams are disregarded when it describes dreams as follows: "Dreams are abnormal and sometimes pathological.... The Bible, contrary to a notion perhaps too commonly held, attaches relatively little religious significance to dreams."[14]

No wonder why.

---

13. Letters of St. Augustine, 1026–1027.
14. George Robinson, "dream." In *International Standard Bible Encyclopedia*, ed. James Orr, n.p., 1915. http://www.biblestudytools.com/encyclopedias/isbe/.

We've seen that, especially in children, dreams can be more "normal" than not dreaming. While some dreams can indeed be soulish or demonic in origin, we've also seen that God has used dreams and visions to communicate significant messages throughout the Bible and humanity. Moreover, since the 1970s, scientific research has shown that lucid dreaming, specifically, is a beneficial reality. Some scientists are even helping people enter into it.

Dr. Stephen LaBerge asks why more people are not dreaming lucidly:

> Lucid dreaming represents...what ought to be a normal ability in adults. If this is correct, why are lucid dreams so rare, especially in cases such as nightmares, where lucidity should be extremely helpful and rewarding?
>
> I think a possible answer can be seen by comparing lucid dreaming with another cognitive skill—language. All normal adults speak and understand at least one language. But how many would do so if they were never taught? Unfortunately, in this culture, with few exceptions, we are not taught to dream.

LaBerge has demonstrated that lucid dreaming is a learnable skill.[15]

If we studied and understood what the holy Scriptures say about dreams and what science says about lucid dreams—both of which are not bound by time, space, or logic—just imagine the great damage we could do to the kingdom of darkness and how we could grow in authority over it. As we gain this authority, we would also gain more control over our dreams.

Some may say, "Isn't lucid dreaming dangerously close to New Age and occult practices?" The answer depends on your motivation

---

15. Stephen LaBerge, "Lucid dreaming: Psychophysiological studies of consciousness during REM sleep" in Sleep and Cognition, eds. R.R. Bootzen, et al. (Washington, D.C.: American Psychological Association, 1990), 122, http://www.lucidity.com/ LaBerge1990-Lucid_Dreaming=Psychophysiological_ Studies_ of_Consciousness_during_REM_Sleep.pdf.

and your teacher. If your motivation is to perform spiritual warfare and fulfill righteousness—and if your teacher is the Word of God and the Holy Spirit—then the answer is no.

But if your motivation is to fulfill your soulish mind, will, or emotions—or if you turn to New Age spiritists, gurus, warlocks and the like to develop your spiritual enlightenment—then the answer is a definite *yes.*

In one of the dream courses that I taught, a lady shared that she is able to rewind her dreams any time she wants while still dreaming. And yes, she is a born–again, God-fearing Christian. When her son was eighteen years old, she dreamt that he and his friend were driving in his car and had a head on collision with another vehicle. She stopped the dream, rewound it, and started over—this time, when the car was about to have a head-on collision, she screamed and pushed the car over three feet with her hand. Then she woke up.

In the dream, she exercised her authority.

Not long after, she got the dreaded call that is every parent's worst nightmare: "This is the police. Your son has been in an accident."

She rushed out the door and drove to the scene. When she get there, the jaws of life were cutting the boys out of the car. The officer told the mom, "I don't know what happened here, but if the car was turned only three feet this way, it would have been a head-on collision and killed the boys."

Through her experience we see that we can change the outcome of spiritual warfare. That's the power of lucid dreaming.

But what normally happens when we have a nightmare? We wake up and are gripped with fear. Our children, when they were little, typically ran to our bedroom trying to tell us through their tears how afraid they were to go back to sleep because they just had a scary dream.

Not to be too repetitive but, at this point, most parents who don't understand dreams will tell their children, "Oh, it was just a dream, Honey. You don't have to be afraid. It's just your imagination." The child will say in their subconscious, "It's not safe to dream," so they shut down their dream life.

I can't tell you how many people I have met come up to me after I teach on this subject to say that is exactly what happened to them: "I was afraid to go to sleep, so I shut down my dream life." Or "I made a choice not to remember my dreams upon waking." Others are continually tormented by their nightmares and sleep with the light on or in their parents' bed.

No matter what age you are, what you fear is what you empower. The more you fear a thing, the more you come into agreement with it in your life. This is what the enemy wants to accomplish in your life and your child's life. This is what he was trying to do in the life of a boy named Corey (names have been changed), as you'll read in his mom's email to me and my response to her:

Dear Recie,

I was hoping I could talk with you or at least gather more resources to help me understand why my son struggles with fear.

I called Streams Ministries for prayer because for the last three years, my son has rarely slept an entire night in his own bed. This has been a journey for our entire family and we have made some progress, but I'm at a loss as to what to do next.

My son, Corey, seems to be more sensitive to the spiritual world than most people. He has seen an angel three times in our home—the first time was when he was six. Soon after that, the bad dreams and scary visions started. He has seen "naked people with tails" and a large snake with a human face. He also described one scary vision as the "black wizard witch." On the positive side, he had a dream that two angels came with swords and slashed through an army of zombies that were outside our house. Cool!

My husband and I are both born-again Christians. We were raised in the church and our parents are born-again Christians. We are active members of our current church. (I actually run the children's ministry.)

Three years ago, at the beginning of this journey, I was begging God to give me insight as to why my son was so fearful. God clearly spoke to me and said, "Get the Bibles from your husband's grandparents out of your house." He and I had been given boxes of keepsakes after his mother passed away. In the boxes there were two Bibles with the Free Masonry symbol on them, previously belonging to his grandparents. We knew Free Masonry was bad, but we justified keeping them because the symbols were on Bibles.

Upon hearing what the Lord said, I immediately took the Bibles outside and burnt them. Again I asked God for more insight, and He said to sort through the papers in the hope chest that had been given to us. I went through the papers and found a Free Masonry diploma in a leather case and other Free Masonry items. Needless to say, I burnt those too.

That evening when my husband came home, I told him what had happened, and we asked the Lord to forgive us for keeping those Free Masonry Bibles. Then we went into every room of our house and walked around the outside and claimed it for Christ. Amazingly, my son slept all night in his room—but it only lasted a few months.

We have had a few other "demonic issues" that God revealed to us, and we prayed it out of our house and have seen wonderful results. Over the years my husband and I have prayed for Corey hundreds of times. We have claimed Bible verses over him. We've had Bible study groups across the country pray for him, hands have been laid on him; tongues have been spoken over him. And yet, this issue of fear still lingers.

We are aware of curses and their negative effects on people and families. We broke the Free Masonry curse. I'm not sure what else to do.

Recie, can you help me? Would you be able to talk with me to help me know what to do for my son? Or maybe you could recommend a book or an article for me to read. I am searching for wisdom.

May the Lord bless you and your ministry!

This was my response to her email:

If children understand—if their eyes are open to the coexisting spiritual realm so that they see the demon or spirit—it means they have authority over it. Remember that Jesus never went after demons by walking around and shouting rebukes into the air. Only when they manifested (when He actually saw them) did He cast them out or say, "Depart from me!"

This story will make my point: Since 1984, I had wanted to meet a man named Bob Jones, who has a strong prophetic voice. In 2007 I finally got a chance to do that, so I took my wife and three kids up to the Carolinas to meet with him: my oldest son, Li'l Recie, was eight years old at the time, and I was teaching him how to see in the Spirit. I had been telling him to ask the Lord to show him animals over people heads and I would help him interpret that image.

At the meeting, I was listening to Bob talk with us when Li'l Recie came up to me and whispered in my ear, "Dad, I have a word for Bob Jones."

I looked at him and said, "Recie, go sit down. I am having a discussion with Bob."

After sitting with Bob for a few minutes, Recie came back up to me and whispered in my ear again, "Dad, I have a word for Bob Jones."

Again I said, "Recie, go sit down. This is my time." I turned my attention back to Bob. Then a third time, Recie came to me and said, "Dad, I have a word for Bob Jones."

This time I perceived it was of the Lord, so I said, "Excuse me Bob but my son, Li'l Recie, has a word for you. Bob smiled and asked, "What is it?"

Li'l Recie said, "I see a tarantula over your head."

To my amazement, Bob replied, "That is exactly the thing that has been wakening me up every morning at 4 a.m. and harassing me in my dreams. None of us saw it, but you saw it. God opened your eye to see it in the Spirit, and that means you have authority over it. Now come over here and pray for me that it would leave and stop its assignment."

Wow, that day I understood a principle in the Spirit realm: If you see a dark spirit, it means you have authority over it. You can then throw the purchased blood of Christ over it and ask it to leave. It has to respond to you.

Likewise, your son needs to understand that if he sees it, he has authority over it. Instead of responding to fear, he can respond to faith and authority in Christ. Two more important principles to understand are:

1. What you focus on, you make room for. Therefore, he needs to ask God to help him see good angels.

2. What you fear, you empower. Fear and faith have the same definition: They both believe that something that has not happened is going to happen.

Your son needs to come out of agreement with fear and understand he has a spiritual gift to see and a spiritual power of authority. He also needs to understand that the enemy's goal is to make him fearful in order to shut his gift down.

It is when you and your child exercise your authority in Christ that each of you breaks your agreement with fear in your life. So how do you do that? We will talk more about that next.

CONTROLLING THE GAME

A few years ago, as I was praying about lucid dreaming and children, the Lord had me connect it to the PlayStation. I thought about how kids are able to control their characters in video games, and in lucid dreams they can do the same. About two years ago, I sat down with my boys to have this very discussion. Both Michael Ray and Li'l Recie had been having nightmares, and I knew what they needed to hear.

I started out by reminding them of the power they have and who is really in control: "You can do anything in a dream through the power of God," I told them. "But right now, when you're having a nightmare and get scared you wake up, right?"

They nodded.

"So you never finish the nightmare and sometimes it comes back."

They nodded some more.

Then I explained how they could take control in their dreams: "It's a lot like when you are playing video games. In the game, you control your character. And in a dream, you can do anything through the power of God. You can even change the direction of your dreams; all you have to do is pick up a stick and whack the bad guys on the head. Or you can turn into Superman and fly away." That made them happy.

"Cool! You can do that?" they asked.

"Sure you can," I said. And they believed me.

As adults we lose out on so much of what God has for us because we haven't experienced it before. We close ourselves off from spiritual encounters. Fortunately, our children are not bound by our experiences or lack thereof. They see with different eyes. My boys believe me—they have no reason to doubt when I tell them something. And they have no reason to doubt their authority in Christ.

Michael Ray fought four bears (see chapter 8) just a month after having this discussion. For Li'l Recie, it took two years to exercise such authority. When he was eight, he told me about a dream of being in a dark, scary place where he was afraid. Instead of waking up and out of the dream, he remembered what I had told him—that he could control his actions and change the direction of them. In his dream he told himself, "My dad said I could turn into Superman and fly," and so he did. He flew out of the dark place and landed on a rock.

Immediately, Jesus came to Recie and said, "Because you exercised your authority over evil, I have a reward and want to show you something." Then Jesus took him to heaven! Recie said that heaven is so bright with colors—the trees, flowers, and grass are all alive and they greeted him. A very nice angel took him to see his mansion—remember, he is only eight and doesn't know there is a verse in the Bible about Jesus preparing a place for us with mansions. He said his mansion was not completed because they were just starting to build it.

Then Jesus told him, "Good–bye, I'll see you again soon." For years he had been asking me what heaven was like, so you can imagine how excited he was when he woke up. Also imagine that he may have never experienced heaven if we had not had that talk about lucid dreams and the power of God to change things.

Many of us parents and our children are missing awesome encounters because when we have a nightmare we wake up instead of staying in the encounter and exercising our authority over fear and evil. Or we try to win in some way, but we feel the enemy resist us in the dream and we flee.

I believe that God allows the enemy to resist us even at a young age so that we can learn how to exercise our authority. We exercise our physical muscles when we have resistance and the same is true for our spiritual muscles.

Taking this concept to the masses, on several occasions as I have ministered around the world, I have asked pastors to gather all the children (five and up) and teenagers in a room so I can speak to them. I begin by talking to them about their favorite video games. We talk about having fun, devising strategy, and developing teamwork, which some games are very good at doing. I am all for those benefits of gaming as long as they are set within a wholesome story or context. Not everything new is bad and not everything old is good. My generation grew up with the TV show *Gilligan's Island*. Every week, we watched a group of stranded people with various skills, talents, and gifts continuously fail to get off their island. What did that teach us kids?

I also talk about cartoons; when my kids were young, I knew all the cartoons at that time. To one group of children, I retold an episode about Jimmy Neutron where Carl, his friend, was having nightmares. He was afraid of llamas, so Jimmy Neutron built a device that could enter Carl's dream and help him overcome his fear. What a powerful episode. All the kids remembered watching it, so we discussed it. I told them, "Just like Carl, you can overcome bad dreams, and the Lord will help you."

Then I asked, "Is anyone having a bad dream?"

I picked on someone to share their dream. We talked about how through God's power—and because they are children of God—they can control those dreams just like they can control their character in a video game. They all got excited. I asked, "What would you do differently in this bad dream if it were your dream?" They each gave some great answers. It was so much fun.

Stop for a moment and ask yourself, "Am I having a bad dream?" If so, what would you like to do differently in it now that you know you can control your actions in it?

After leading one of these discussions, I received an email from a mother who was listening with her five-year-old son. She said, "When you came to speak, I didn't even think my son was listening to you. But one night he woke up and said he was having a nightmare or bad dream, and in the dream he said, 'That bald man with hair on his chin [that would be me] said I could get a gun and shoot the bad guy.' Then he told me, 'And I did, Mommy, and that bad guy ran away.'"

It encouraged me again to know that kids believe me, but I'm still discouraged that so many parents struggle with what I say because they have unresolved fear issues or are still stuck with some theological issue, and they can't get free.

Another parent who listened to me talk to children about this said, "I really didn't believe you, but that night I had a bad dream. In the dream, I was afraid and felt like I was about to wake myself up. A PlayStation control popped up in my dream, and I was able to control my dream and exercise my authority over evil." This is possible because dreams and other activities in the spirit world are not bound by logic, time, or space.

This truth can easily be applied to even our mundane lives. For instance, have you had a day when certain people bugged you, and you couldn't pinpoint why you were so frustrated and irritated at them? It is very possible that in your dream that night, God wanted to show you what you could not see in the natural realm— that is, he wanted to show you what was going on in the spirit realm with these people and you. In the dream, you would have had the opportunity to exercise your authority over the spiritual issue and gain freedom.

This happened when I was preparing for a trip to Israel. It was about a week out and I was moody, frustrated, quick to fly off the handle with my wife and kids. A few days before I was about to leave, my wife had a dream: At the doorway to our bedroom stood a demon who said, "We are going to kill Recie. We will follow him all the way to Israel and kill him." Then she woke up.

Too many times, Christians freak out at their encounters with demons instead of realizing the enemy is showing his hand—that is, openly sharing with us what he wants to do to us or what he wants from us, which allows us to effectively pray against it. My wife and I prayed with authority for protection, received the victory, and accomplished all that God had for me in Israel.

That was ten years ago, and I'm still here.

REPETITIVE LUCID DREAMS

Another form of lucid dreaming is experiencing the same dream again and again. This next illustration will sound wild but, in truth, it illustrates the power of God working through us. We only need to understand how to access it:

Both my sons woke up one morning to tell me about their dream. Recie said, "Last night we had a dream, and in the dream we saw one of our friends, and he was being attacked by these mean, evil-looking monsters. So me and Michael Ray ran over and started helping him fight off these bad guys. We beat them up and won."

I said, "Wow, you both had the same dream?" They said, "Yep."

"I bet your friend had the same dream," I told them. "When you go to school, ask him."

They came home from school so excited: "Dad! He had the same exact dream!"

That is the power of lucid dreaming. Recie and Michael Ray fought evil in the spiritual realm—their dreams—to help their friend who was having some scary spiritual warfare happening in his own life.

To exercise this kind of authority over evil, it is critical that we teach our children who they are in Christ, and who their Father is, so that they can begin to build strength for the spiritual battle ahead. To do this, we as Christian parents must become familiar with the workings of the spiritual realm and recapture the authority the enemy has stolen from us so that we can pass this treasure on to our kids.

10

Raising Up a Great Generation

In reading about the last days, there is one passage in particular that struck me as very odd. Jesus said this about mothers during the horrific condition of the days to come:

> Woe to those who are pregnant and to those who are nursing babies in those days; for there will be great distress upon the land and wrath to this people; and they will fall by the edge of the sword, and will be led captive into all the nations; and Jerusalem will be trampled under foot by the Gentiles until the times of the Gentiles are fulfilled. (Luke 21:23–24)

I wondered for months why Jesus would give a warning for nursing and pregnant women and not for women who already have lots of children. So I asked God for insight and meditated on the Word. While doing so, I considered the context of the chapter: the destruction of Israel.

But what does a nursing mother have to do with Israel? Since I interpret dreams, I looked at the statement as a metaphor. In Scripture we often see that women are likened to the church. As believers, we are referred to as the bride of Christ, for whom He is returning as our Bridegroom. (See, for example, Mark 2:39.) We also know that milk is used in Scripture to refer to teaching that is elementary or basic. (See Hebrews 5:12–13.)

So I thought, *Perhaps God is saying, "Woe to those women—or churches—who are still breastfeeding their children. When the darkness and the deception comes on the earth, your children will still be drinking milk and will be deceived because they will not be able to understand how the spirit realm works."*

I talked with well-known theologian R. T. Kendall about my thoughts on this passage, and he said that I could surely take that liberty and read it as a metaphor. So, in applying that metaphor to the reality of the church—the bride of Christ—we see how seeker-sensitive churches have been breastfeeding their seekers. They do this by giving messages on how to fulfill their soulish desires instead of on the more advanced and necessary topics of how the spirit realm operates or their true purpose in it. They keep their seeker-children locked up in a dark box of ignorance or misunderstanding—and declare them to be children of light!

The result is that the world—including New Age, Wicca, and other false religions—know more about the spirit realm of dreams, visions, and mystic and lucid dreaming than the church does! And that knowledge attracts our children. This is a disturbing reality, especially because their knowledge and understanding comes from a dark spirit and not from the light of God.

YOUR EARTHLY ASSIGNMENT

We have been given a great earthly assignment—to train up our children in the way they should go. (See Proverbs 22:6.) To help us do this with regard to hearing God through dreams visions and angelic encounters, we must search out and discover the lost things of God's kingdom and restore them to His people. We must set a new standard for our children by demonstrating to them how to walk in the Lord's Spirit and not the world's spirit.

The enemy is after our children. He wants to destroy their spiritual gifts and he's holding nothing back. It is our job, as parents, to train our children to hear God over the influx of occult media, books, and games. We've seen how He wants to communicate with them in many ways, but we have often put emphasis on the milk of the Word—teaching only the basics about Jesus, salvation, and baptism. We take our children to Sunday school and teach them to pray and to be kind to one another—and rightly so. These things are foundational. But now is the time for the meat.

Our children must hear their God in order to become who He is calling them to be and to be able to stand against the wiles of the devil. They must learn to understand God's many languages and know that He desires to communicate with them. Even children as young as four years old are experiencing God's dreams and visions, seeing angels, and having God-encounters. They need our wisdom and guidance in order to step into their calling.

It's time we taught our children about the night seasons and the power of God to work in their lives whether asleep or awake. It is our destiny to prepare this generation in spiritual matters so that they in turn can fulfill their destiny of becoming the greatest, most spiritually alive generation ever.

MY HEART

I pray that this dream guide has helped you and given you some understanding and guidance for your life, for your children's or grandchildren's lives, and for those you have influence over. I also pray you will study all the Scriptures in the Bible relating to a dream or vision or angelic encounter. There is lots of false teaching regarding this subject, so trust the Holy Spirit and stay updated with our media and resources at dreamschildren.com.

Thank you so much for reading the book that John Paul Jackson told me to write twelve years ago.

Love and blessings, Recie.

Dream Dictionary

You probably have lots of questions about what something in a dream symbolizes. For instance, what does a house mean? What does a dog mean? What does a Sponge Bob mean? In learning to interpret what a dream means, look at each person or thing as a metaphor in which one thing is the same as a totally unrelated thing.

The first step in interpreting symbols is to ask God to speak to you and make the dream clear.

Next, if there is a particular person or thing in the dream like Sponge Bob, look up his characteristics and what he is known for. This could help you understand why he is in the dream.

I usually use Google to search for the real or metaphoric characteristics of any animal in the dream. For instance, a snake is called the deceiver in the Bible and is symbolic for a lie or liar.

This Dream Dictionary is far from a comprehensive resource for all the people, places, and things that will inhabit your children's dreams. For the most part, it is a list of frequently encountered terms and metaphors that I have experienced in my ministry with dreamers.

I will be positing more tips and answering questions from readers about interpretations of symbols at dreamschildren.com.

BODY PARTS

Arm: strength, faith

Beard: maturity

Hair: wisdom and anointing

Hand: relationship; direction

Nakedness: humility; without guile; transparency

Neck: stiff-necked; stubborn, obstinate

Nose: discernment

Paralyzation of body parts: some sort of spiritual hindrance; under demonic attack

Side: area of vulnerability; a place of friendship, relationship

Thigh: faith

Teeth: wisdom, comprehension, understanding

Teeth—Eye teeth: revelatory understanding; to see and understand

Wisdom teeth: wisdom; ability to act in wisdom

COLORS

Black and white: typically bad dreams

Bright colors: dreams in full bright color are from God

Muted colors: dreams in muted color are produced from your soul

Blue: revelation, sadness

Green: growth, envy

Orange: stick with it, don't quit, stubbornness

Purple: authority

Red: wisdom, anointing power

Yellow: gifts, hope, fear, pride

CREATURES

Alligator: aggressive, pushy; large mouth; attacks with mouth, defends with tail

Bear: judgment; strength

Bee/hornet: painful, strong demonic attack

Cat: independent thinking, willful

Cat—Black cat: witchcraft; familiar spirit

Dog: dogs are typically man's best friend, so in a dream, a dog could symbolize a find the child personally knows.

Donkey: gentle strength, burden bearer, can be stubborn

Eagle: prophetic; prophetic calling

Elephant: great impact; big issue

Fly/Flies: occult activity; lives off dead things (*Lord of the Flies*)

Frog: lust

Goat: no discernment (will eat anything); blessings, abundance (context)

Horse: power, can be significant power; a movement of God

Monkey: mockery

Mule: stubbornness

Octopus: Jezebel spirit

Ox/cow: slow change; sustenance

Panther (black): high level witchcraft, occult activity

Polar bear: note color; context is important

Rat: feeds on garbage/impurities (sin); creature of darkness

Sheep: humility; submission; sacrifice; prosperity, responsibility (context)

Snake: a long "tale"; lies.

Snake—Large or venomous: more destructive

Snake—White snake: spirit of religion; occult

Spider: occult attack

Spider web: place of demonic attack; trap

Tiger: soul power

Whale: similar to "elephant", emphasizing things of Spirit

Wolf: false authority, false teaching; picks on the weak

OBJECTS OR IMPLEMENTS

Clothing: It is important to note the color of clothing items.

Clothing—Coat: mantle; anointing

Clothing—Culturally specific clothing: calling to another country; intercession for a foreign land

Clothing—Ragged or poorly fitting: walking in something you are not called into

Clothing—Shoes: peace; gospel of peace

Clothing—Shorts: walk or calling only being partially fulfilled

Clothing—Speedo: to move fast in the spirit

Clothing—Swimwear: ability to move in the spirit, to go deep

Clothing—Wedding dress: covenant; deep relationship

Ring: covenant; authority

Weapon: If the dreamer is holding/using the weapon, it's for battle or a form of protection.

Weapon—Knife: If the dreamer is being attacked, it refers to a verbal attack, gossip, communication issues.

Weapon—Sword: similar to "knife" but further reaching, more influence or effectiveness; authority; the Word

Weapon—Gun: spiritual authority, either good or bad

Weapon—Dart: curses; demonic attack; accuracy

STRUCTURES

Amphitheater: something is going to be magnified

Auto repair shop: minister/ministry restoration, renewal, repair

Castle: authority, fortress, royal residence (where the King lives)

Country general store: serene, basics, staples

Farm: place of provision, learn to grow

Gas station: to receive power

Hospital: healing

Hotel: transition; temporary; relax and receive

House: a ministry, church, or personal life situation

House (two-story): double anointing

House—Living in the house of a known person in the ministry: represents that God has a similar call on your life as that of the other person.

Mall: the "marketplace; provision for all of your needs in one place; in the negative, materialism, self-centeredness

Mobile home: temporary place and condition

Office building: look at size and purpose; calling or gifting

Skyscrapers/high-rise buildings: high spiritual calling

Shack: poverty or on holiday, vacation (context)

Stadium: tremendous impact

Tent: temporary, but can lead to permanent

Barn/Warehouse: place of provision, storage, where you can find what you need

Theater: you're going to be shown something

STRUCTURES/ROOMS IN A HOUSE

Atrium: light and growth from heaven

Attic: history, past issues; stored things (dusty)

Basement: hidden issues

Bathroom: cleansing, spiritual toxins removed

Bedroom: intimacy; rest

Dining room/eating: partaking of spiritual food; fellowship; receiving spiritual things

Elevator: rising or descending of anointing

Foundation: important foundational issues

Garage: rest, refreshing, stored for some use later

Garden: love and intimacy (Eden/Paradise, Song of Solomon); growth

Hallway: transition, direct and without deviation

In public: humility; God doing a work in you that everyone will know about, but this will be a preparation process for promotion and use.

Kitchen: preparing spiritual food

Porch—Back: history

Porch—Front: vision, future

Restaurant kitchen: greater influence/impact

Roof: spiritual covering

Staircase: up or down in the Spirit; can be a portal (context)

Windows: vision; letting light in

TRANSPORTATION

Vehicles generally have to do with ministry or vocation.

Airplane: able to go to heights in the spirit; church, ministry, corporation; a movement—the larger the movement the greater the impact; referring to influencing people in the spiritual arena. If it's on the ground, it's not ready to take off yet.

Armored car: the protection of God

Automobile: personal ministry; job

Bicycle: individual ministry or calling; requires perseverance, commitment. Remember, a "riding a bicycle" dream today does not mean that will always be the case. They could be flying a 747 jetliner next month.

Bus: church or ministry

Cars—Convertible: open heaven

Cars—Fred Flintstone car: human effort

Cars—Limousine: the call of God on your life; being taken to your destiny (but note context)

Cars—Mickey Mouse car: a purpose that is colorful and entertaining

Cars—Taxi cab: driving could be referring to a hireling (e.g., shepherd vs. a hireling); riding have to pay the price in order to get where you're going

Chariot: if taking you from earth to heaven, a major spiritual encounter; life destiny

Fire truck: (note context) rescue, put out fire of destruction; or, put out the fire of the spirit (note color, or lack of)

Helicopter: mobile, flexible, able to get in the spirit quickly

Motorcycle: fast, powerful, maneuverable

Rollercoaster: exciting, but temporary thrill

Semi-truck, 18-wheeler: transporting large amounts, on assignment; partial (semi)

Ships/Boats—Ocean liner: impacting large numbers of people

Ships/Boats—Riverboat: on the river of life, slow, impacting many people, joyous

Ships/Boats—Sailboat: fast, powered by the wind (Holy Spirit); in the water—influence with people and in the spirit

Ships/Boats—Speedboat: fast, exciting, power in the spirit

Ships/Boats—Tug boat: vital assistance; ministry of helps

Ships/Boats—Submarine: undercover, active, but not seen by many

Spaceship: to the outer limits spiritually

Stagecoach: rough, difficult ride but will get where going

Subway: same as "submarine"

Tow truck: ministry of helps; gathers wounded

Tractor: slow, power, need to plow

Truck; pick-up truck: (note word play) to "pick up" something to transport, deliver to

Train: a movement of God

WEATHER/NATURAL OCCURANCES

Clouds: same principle as "storms"

Earthquake: judgment; a shaking

Rain: if it is clear from God (His Spirit raining down); if it is dark or filthy, from the enemy

Snow: righteousness, refreshing

Storm: if light, they are from God; if dark, they are from the enemy; trouble, turbulence

Tornado/Hurricane: same principle as "storms"

Wind: the Holy Spirit; or in the negative, adversity

PROBING QUESTIONS ABOUT THE DREAM

A. Is the person in the dream known to the dreamer?

1. **How are they connected to the dreamer?** Family, church, job, past, etc.

2. **What is the person's name in the dream?** A person's name can have great significance to their purpose in

the dream, and, thus, to the meaning of the dream. Refer to books that give the biblical and historical derivation of names.

3. **What stands out about them?** Was there something distinct about their actions? Was there some physical quality that was exaggerated?

4. **What does the person portray in the dreamer's life?** Is it the literal person or do they represent something (e.g., John Paul and the prophetic)?

5. **What spiritual quality do they portray?** Do they portray something positive or negative? Do they exude peace, joy, love, kindness, etc.? They could represent the spiritual quality they portray.

6. **Does the dreamer like, dislike, or is neutral toward them?**

7. **Has this person appeared in other dreams?** Understanding can be gained by what purpose they served in the other dreams.

B. Is this a person unknown to the dreamer?

1. **How would they be described?** Physical qualities, clothing, items they are holding.

2. **From their actions or manner, what name could they be given?**

3. **What role do they play in the dream?** What feeling or tone does this person add to the dream? What percentage of the dream is impacted by this person?

4. **4. Does the person exude any qualities?** Positive or negative?

C. Faceless people

1. Is the person's countenance dark or light?

2. What feeling or tone does this person exude or add to the dream?

3. Does this person seem to hinder or help the dream's direction? This may reveal whether the person is good or bad.

4. Does the person display any special powers or heavenly qualities? This may reveal them as an angel or merely a person. Faceless persons that display positive spiritual qualities, heavenly power, or authority are often angels. On occasion they can represent the Holy Spirit or the Lord Jesus. Faceless persons that display the opposite qualities are often demonic. Angels in dreams will glorify God, minister His purposes, and point to Jesus.

D. Named persons

1. The name may be the meaning of the dream. The name of the person or the position they hold can be a metaphor for the meaning of the dream.

2. Is the name in Scripture?

3. Their name may be a prophetic pointer to what is going to happen.

4. The name of the position they hold, or represent, is significant. Note political and spiritual leaders. For example, a president or king

Dream Journal

WHAT DOES THAT MEAN?

You probably have a lot of questions about what something in a dream symbolizes. For instance, what does a house mean? What does a dog mean? What does a Sponge Bob mean? For specific details within the dream, refer to the Dream Dictionary I've included in this book. In learning to interpret what a dream means, look at each person or thing in the dream as a metaphor that represents an overarching theme or message from God.

When my children were young, I didn't have a special dream journal to keep their dreams safe. I used a regular notebook. I printed their names and taped their pictures on the front. My kids loved them. Every morning after they had a dream, they would bring their dream journals to me and we would record what they heard and saw and felt in the dream. Sometimes we drew pictures of their dreams, but many times we just wrote them down. Even if we didn't know what the dream meant, we still talked to the Lord about how we loved Him for talking to us in our dreams.

I encourage you to begin using this dream journal to chronicle the communication your children are receiving from God as they sleep. Keep things simple and fun. Draw pictures. Turn them into stories. Don't get frustrated if you can't figure all the dreams out right away. The important thing is to record as many details as possible before they are forgotten and lost. Over time, you may begin to sense certain themes and messages the rise to the surface. As a parent, you may need to take time to pray that God would give you revelation for what certain dreams mean.

After three or four months of recording dreams, you'll have fun going back to the beginning of the journal and re-reading the dreams. In doing this, many times, parents and children will experience a breakthrough, and say, "Oh, that's what that dream meant!"

I hope you enjoy your dream life and time spent talking with your children about our amazingly creative God.

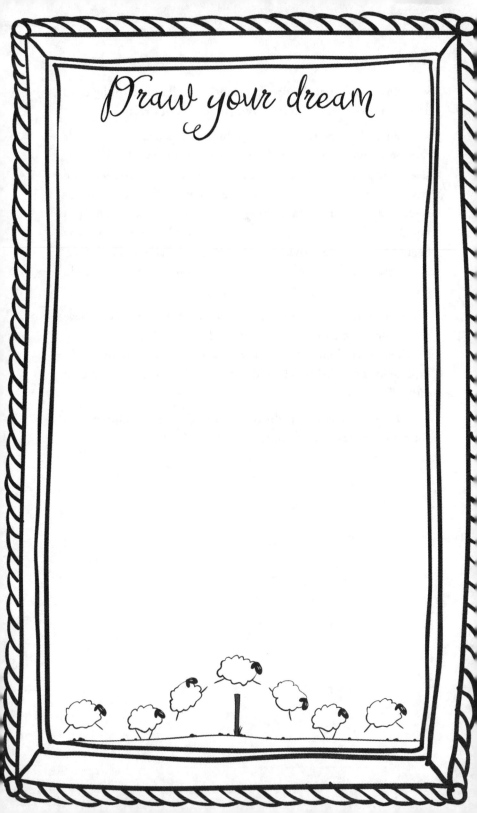

Draw your dream

TITLE YOUR DREAM _____

DATE _____

Write your dream

_____
_____
_____
_____
_____
_____
_____
_____
_____
_____
_____
_____
_____

PARENTS' NOTES •

_____
_____
_____
_____

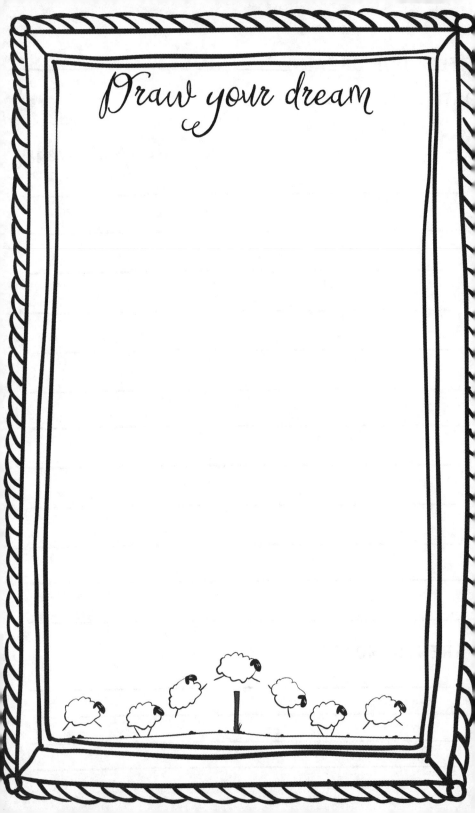

Draw your dream

TITLE YOUR DREAM _____

DATE _____

Write your dream

_____
_____
_____
_____
_____
_____
_____
_____
_____
_____
_____
_____

PARENTS' NOTES •

_____
_____
_____
_____

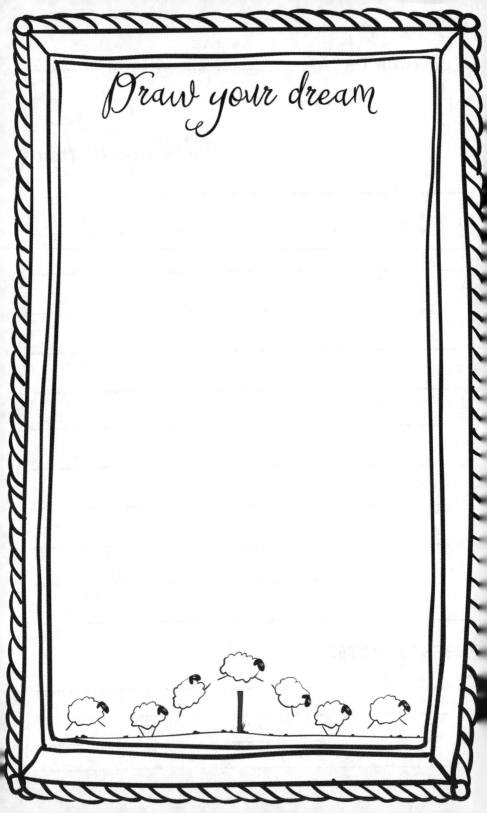

Draw your dream

TITLE YOUR DREAM _____

DATE _____

Write your dream

_____
_____
_____
_____
_____
_____
_____
_____
_____
_____
_____
_____
_____
_____

PARENTS' NOTES •

_____
_____
_____
_____

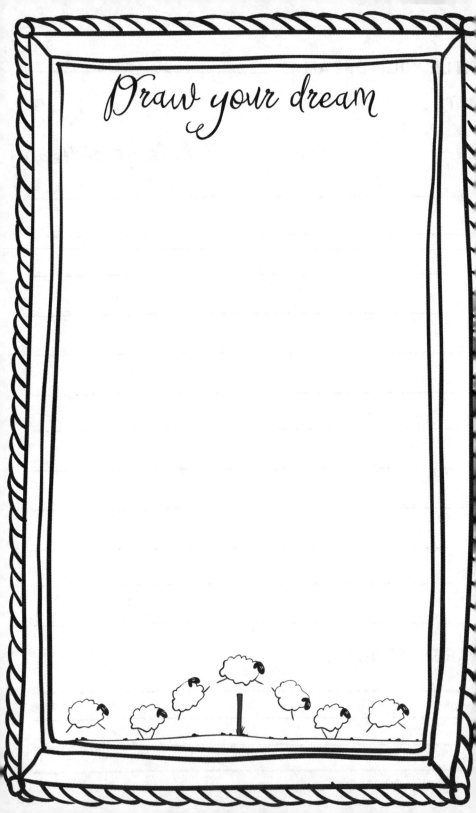
Draw your dream

TITLE YOUR DREAM _____

DATE _____

Write your dream

_____

_____

_____

_____

_____

_____

_____

_____

_____

_____

_____

_____

PARENTS' NOTES •

_____

_____

_____

_____

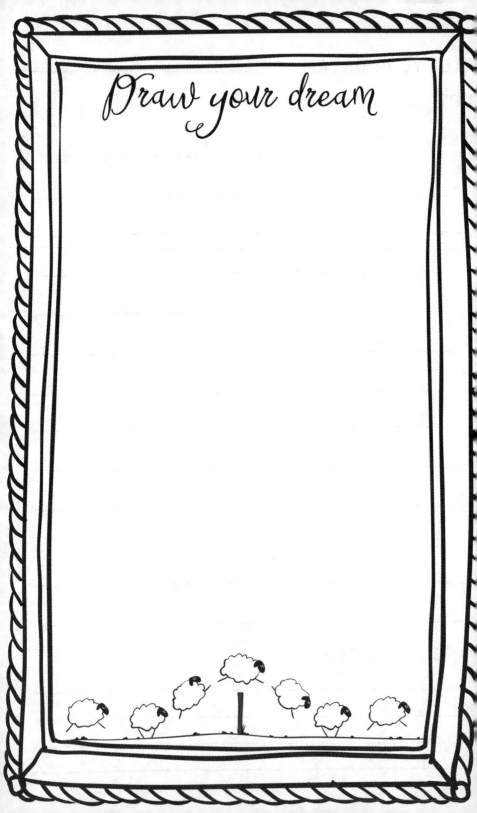

Draw your dream

TITLE YOUR DREAM _____

DATE _____

Write your dream

_____
_____
_____
_____
_____
_____
_____
_____
_____
_____
_____
_____
_____

PARENTS' NOTES •

_____
_____
_____
_____

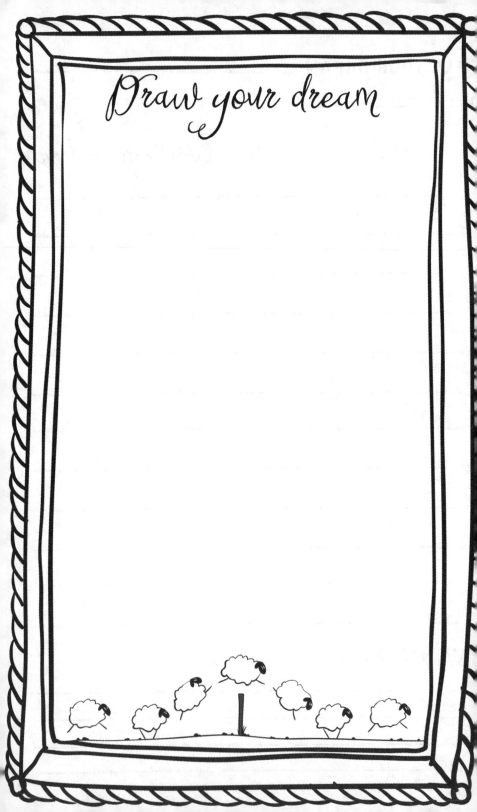

Draw your dream

TITLE YOUR DREAM _____

DATE _____

Write your dream

_____
_____
_____
_____
_____
_____
_____
_____
_____
_____
_____
_____
_____

PARENTS' NOTES •

_____
_____
_____
_____

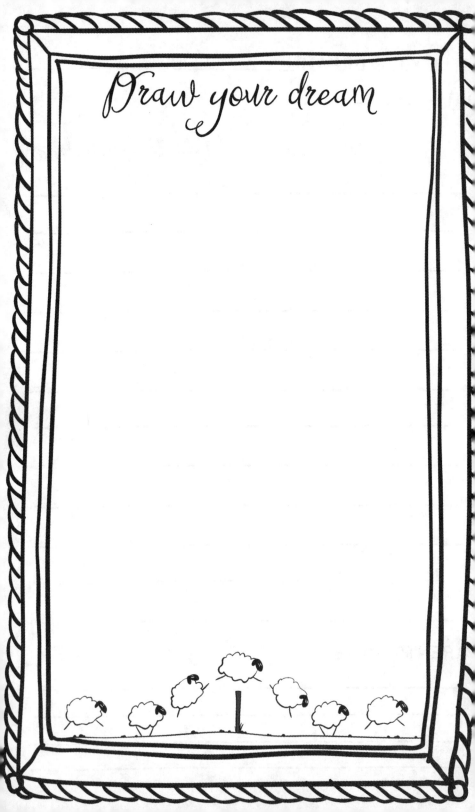

Draw your dream